International Poetry Review

VOLUME 47 | 2024

GUEST EDITOR
Suja Sawafta, U of Miami

EDITOR
Ana Hontanilla, UNC Greensboro

ASSOCIATE EDITOR
Rose Facchini, Tufts U

FOUNDING EDITOR
Evalyn Pierpoint Gill

WEBSITE MANAGER
Joshua Lunsford

Founded in 1975 by Evalyn Pierpoint Gill, *International Poetry Review* is dedicated to the idea that the world becomes a better place when we stop to explore and listen to the voices of writers in diverse languages and from different cultures. This journal publishes works by contemporary writers in all languages, with facing English translations. *International Poetry Review* is of interest to anyone who loves the rhythms and beauty of the written word in all languages.

Acknowledgements

A sincere thanks is owed to the translators, writers, editors, and publishers who collectively made this work possible. Without them, and their love for poetry and translation, this issue would not be possible.

International Poetry Review counts among its lifelong supporters the following poetry lovers:

Louis Bourne
Phil Cohen
Fred and Susan Chappell
Bernhard Frank
Alice Hill
Ruthie Katzenstein
Stevenson Lupton, Jr.
Karol Neufeld
David Schenck, Ph.D.
Maria H. Schilke
Dr. Alan E. Smith
David and Zita Smith
Mrs. Betty Watson

Special thanks to the Office of Research and Engagement and the International Program Center Kohler Fund at the University of North Carolina Greensboro and to the office of the Senior Associate Dean for Research and Graduate Education at the University of Miami for supporting the publication of this issue.

The *International Poetry Review* is published annually by the Department of Languages, Literatures, and Cultures at UNC Greensboro. The journal was previously published twice a year through Volume 42, Numbers 1 & 2 (Spring & Fall 2016).

Authors who would like to publish their work in English translation and translators who would like to publish their work, please email the editor, Rose Facchini, at rose.facchini@tufts.edu. Please do not send manuscripts by mail.

Annual subscriptions for individuals are available through the Department for $18. A $12 international shipping fee will be added for non-U.S. subscribers. To subscribe, call (336) 334-5655 or email amhontan@uncg.edu. Institutions can subscribe through EBSCO or other agencies for $22.

Copyright © 2024 *International Poetry Review*. All rights reserved.

ISBN: 978-1-4696-7734-7

Cover image: © Furat Sawafta and Chema Castelló, 2023.

Typesetting: codeMantra

Department of
Languages, Literatures,
and Cultures

Contents

10   Letter from the Editor

Arabic

14   **Abul Qassem al-Shabbi**, "إرادة الحياة"
"The Will of Life", Translated by Suja Sawafta

18   **Adonis**, "ليس نجمًا", "آخر السّماء", "شدّاد", and "مرثية الحلّاج"
"No Star", "The Sky's End", "Shaddad", and "Elegy for al-Hallaj", Translated by Kareem James Abu-Zeid and Ivan S. Eubanks

27   **Muhammad al-Saghir Awlad Ahmad**,
"تونسي، دفعة واحدة، أو لا أكون" and "مصعد باتجاه الهاوية"
"Tunisian I am, for once and for all, or else I will not be" and "Ascending towards the Abyss", Translated by Hanan Natour

35   **Nazik al-Mala'ika**, "ثورة على الشّمس" and "أغنية للقمر"
"Revolt Against the Sun" and "A Song for the Moon", Translated by Emily Drumsta

46   **Farah Barqawi**, "كلبة ضالة" and "سؤال العودة"
"Stray" and "The Question of Return", Translated by Katharine Halls

55   **Ramy Essam**, "ارحل"
"Get Out", Translated by Suja Sawafta

59 **Al-Sayyid Mohammad Hussayn Fadlallah**, "شعر بلا عنوان"
"Untitled Poetry", Translated by Alexander Nachman

61 **Jawdat Fakhreddine**, "مختارات من تقاطعات"
"Selections from 'Intersections' by Jawdat Fakhreddine", Translated by Huda Fakhreddine

70 **Adam Fethi**, "نشيد الحياة"
"The Song of Life", Translated by Hager Ben Driss

100 **Sammany Hajo**, "مطالب"
"Matalib", Self-translated by Sammany Hajo

103 **Ameer Hamad**, "صلاة" and "البحر المتوسط"
"The Mediterranean Sea" and "Prayer", Translated by Katharine Halls

107 **Omar Hathiq**, "إذا متّ لا تدفنوني هنا"
"If I Die, Do Not Bury Me Here", Translated by Chihab El Khachab

111 **Nouri al-Jarrah**, "اِحْتِفَالٌ بَهِيمِيٌّ" and "وِشَاحٌ أُرْجُوَانِيٌّ"
"A Brutish Celebration" and "A Purple Scarf", Translated by Allison Blecker

119 **Mona Kareem**, "اعتقال قصيدة" and "مدن تموت يوميًّا"
"Arresting a Poem" and "Cities Dying Every Day", Translated by Sara Elkamel

125 **Rania Mamoun**, "كتابات عن الثورة في السودان ٢٠١٩"
"Selections from *Something Evergreen Called Life*",
Translated by Yasmine Seale

133 **Raja Meziane**, "Allô le Système !"
"Allô le Système !", Self-translated by Raja Meziane

137 **Ibrahim Tuqan**, "موطني"
"My Homeland", Translated by Maha Salah

French

141 **Tahar Bekri**, "Je te dis printemps", "Mûrier dans le printemps arabe", "L'épopée des nus", and "Lampedusa"
"I Tell You Spring", "A Mulberry Tree in the Arab Spring", "The Epic of the Naked", and "Lampedusa", Translated by Khalid Lyamlahy

151 **Ahmed Bouanani**, "L'Analphabète" and "Aux poètes prisonniers"
"The Illiterate Man" and "To the Poet Prisoners", Translated by Emma Ramadan

163 **Hadrien Bureau and Tracy Nehmé**, "Le 17 octobre"
"October 17th", Self-translated by Hadrien Bureau and Tracy Nehmé

169 **Hocine Tandjaoui**, "Extrait de *Clameur*"
"Excerpt from *Clamor*", Translated by Olivia C. Harrison and Teresa Villa-Ignacio

Persian

175 **Ahmad Shamlou**, "در میدان"
"In the Square", Translated by Maziyar Ghiabi

English

177 **George Abraham**, "Taking Back Jerusalem" and "Alternate Myths of Exile"

184 **Zaina Alsous**, "Apologies to All the People in Yemen" and "IBIS"

189 **Hala Alyan**, "The Worst Ghosts" and "Call Me to Prayer"

192 **Sara Elkamel**, "November" and "Drone Fiction"

194 **K. Eltinaé**, "daugterland" and "malexi dawa bay"

197 **Farrah Fray**, "Libya is Blue"

198 **Maziyar Ghiabi**, "A Fidel"

201 **Fady Joudah**, "Calligraphy for a Sagittarius"

204 **Mohja Kahf**, "Hurra bint Hurra" and "The Freedom You Want"

207 **Ismail Khalidi**, "Where This Fire Begins"

212 **Khaled Mattawa**, "OCCUPATION (AN INDEX)"

217 **Omar Offendum**, "I Wish"

219 **Nadya Tannous**, "The Season of the Jasmine Vine"

226 **Lena Khalaf Tuffaha**, "Miss Sahar Completes Her Application for Travel Documents"

230 **Peter Twal**, "People Who Are Trying to Be Polite"

Letter from the Editor

Revolutions are about bread and freedom, the gnawing demands of a physical and spiritual hunger that refuses to relent. Physical and existential survival, the desire to dismantle the conditions that perpetuate suffering and replace them with structures that support life, brought people to the streets in Tunisia in 2010. These are the same forces that lead the disenfranchised and the dreamers of every society to camp outside the palace or presidential gates, claiming a safer, sustainable reality. The inextricable connection between bread and freedom lives on in the urban legend fossilized in our cultural psyche, recounted in history classes on the French Revolution (July 1789-November 1799). It is said that when Marie-Antoinette, the last queen of France, was told that the peasants had no bread, she infamously responded, "Qu'ils mangent de la brioche," or as the phrase has come to be known in English, "Let them eat cake." Though this infamous reaction has been falsely attributed to her, it nonetheless illuminates the zeitgeist that defines any revolution: the gulf between the people on one end and the political elite on the other, the latter often blind to life's hardships and only worried about its preservation and self-interests.

But we must never underestimate the struggles around the food basket or the vegetable cart, as the example set forth by Mohammed Bouazizi taught us. He is the young Tunisian street vendor who self-immolated in December 2010 and subsequently died in January 2011; he was the spark that ignited the Tunisian Revolution, also known as the Jasmine Revolution or the Revolution of Dignity. It is said that Bouazizi worked as a street vendor for most of his twenty-six years of existence. His death was the result of years of maltreatment by the local police in Sidi Bouzid; authorities regularly harassed Bouazizi, demanding bribes and confiscating his wares—a vendor cart and the produce he had purchased through a loan of roughly two hundred dollars—without which he had no way of making an honest living or supporting his mother and siblings. Bouazizi was well-loved and referred to by his neighbors as "Basbousa," a semolina cake soaked in an orange blossom simple syrup; his dignity and kindness prevailed despite his misfortunes, and he was known for feeding those less fortunate from his cart. On the 17th of December 2010, this violent cycle became unbearable. Bouazizi doused himself in gasoline and set himself on fire with a match, a sacrifice that provoked public outrage and a solidarity that, in turn, led to the start of a four-week revolution. Protests ended by mid-January 2011 with the departure of the country's dictator, Zine El Abidine Ben Ali, in power since 1987.

The revolution spread like wildfire into Egypt, where youth activists comparably recalled the death of Khaled Mohamed Saeed, who was beaten to death while in police custody in Sidi Gaber, Alexandria, in June 2010. On the 25th of January 2011, the youth called for a day of protest to coincide with Egypt's national police day, and throughout two weeks and three days, a combined strategy of protest, occupation, nonviolent resistance, and civil disobedience, dissenters managed to overthrow the country's then-incumbent leader, Hosni Mubarak. The revolutions in Tunisia and Egypt ignited what would soon be called "The Arab Spring," a series of revolutions that would expand beyond these two states into Libya, Syria, Yemen, and Bahrain, and smaller protest movements elsewhere in the region.

While Tunisia remained an emblem of hope for the democratic transition process, other countries, notably Libya and Syria, descended into unparalleled violence and chaos. Popular desires in these two places were hijacked by international greed and proxy conflicts, resulting in mass migrations across the Mediterranean. The dream of freedom in Syria is still ongoing, but the price to be paid for this desire is perhaps the dearest. In Palestine, a century of resistance against settler-colonialism and apartheid prevails, and in Algeria and Sudan, traditions of African resistance were revived in manifestations of Arab Spring aftershocks, closing out a decade of protest in the region. More recently (2018-2019), eight months of Sudanese protests led to the ouster of Omar Al-Bashir after three decades in power. The Hirak Movement in Algeria, also known as "The Revolution of Smiles," began less than a week after the country's former president Abdelaziz Bouteflika announced his candidacy for a fifth presidential term, after two decades in power. Voters rejected Bouteflika's announcement and rushed to the streets. In Lebanon, a revolution began in October 2019 when the Lebanese government announced its plans to increase taxes on gasoline, tobacco, and applications such as WhatsApp. The rage of the Lebanese people was only stifled by the coming of the COVID-19 pandemic. Iraq also had its own October between 2019 and 2021, comparable to their Lebanese counterparts, Iraqi civil activists participated in a series of protests against corruption, interventionism, and economic collapse. Each country's range of revolutionary events and activities is as diverse as the cultures, histories, and individuals involved. The governmental responses to these movements, coups, revolutionary hijacking, and interventions, are also numerous and unrelenting. However, two things undoubtedly tie the revolutions of this region together: the demand for freedom and the centrality of poetry.

This issue centers on the role of poetry as a form of protest in Middle Eastern and North African traditions. It opens with the Tunisian poet Abul Qassem al-Shabbi's "The Will of Life," which became the official anthem of Tunisian protestors during the Tunisian Revolution. Though Al-Shabbi lived and died tragically young at age twenty-five, long before the outbreak of the Jasmine Revolution, his poetic legacy and modernizing writing remain undisputed. Two verses from this poem speak to this volume: "If one day people will to live / then fate has no choice but to comply." We feature canonical Mashreqi voices, such as Palestine's Ibrahim Tuqan, Syria's Adonis, and Iraq's Nazik al-Mala'ika, along with emerging poets, who write in Arabic. From the Maghreb, poets such as Ahmed Bouanani, Hocine Tandjaoui, and Tahar Bekri expressed their revolutionary desires and reflections in French. Emerging artists are featured in the Arabic and French sections, but the reader will find that the English section also highlights and centers on the revolutionary angst of the youth. The Editor has taken several creative liberties for inclusion and representation; artists may reside in the Arab world or the diaspora, but all the works are politically inclined regardless of the magnetizing pulls of their linguistic registers, geographic locales, or cultural influences. The number of artists across generations, languages, and revolutionary movements in the last two centuries reminds us that there is great beauty in times of tragedy.

I would be remiss not to mention that music throughout these various revolutionary moments has been an indispensable and influencing factor of popular mobilization. This issue features the lyrics of rappers and singer-songwriters whose songs have become anthems to protest movements in their countries. The lyricists featured alongside these poets include the Egyptian artist Ramy Essam, whose song "Irhal" was first sung in Cairo's Tahrir Square during the January 25th Revolution; Sudanese artist Sammany Hajo, whose song Sudan's 2019 Revolution inspired Matalib and was recently featured in a COLORS x STUDIOS feature on Sudan; Algerian rapper and lawyer Raja Meziane, whose song "Allô le Système !" expressed the rage of the Algerian youth in 2019; and of course Syrian-American artist Omar Offendum, whose work both before and in the aftermath of the Arab Spring offers no shortage of beauty, inspiration, and commitment.

As I write these words in 2023, the political conflict between Palestine and Israel is particularly concerning. Crackdowns against people trying to continue their lives despite military occupation and apartheid increase in brutality. The English language section of this issue showcases some of the best poetry from the Palestinian diaspora and Arab America. In Sudan, rival generals fight for control, leaving millions of citizens as collateral damage. In Iran, protests against the government's morality police and policies of compulsory veiling have raged since late September 2022 after the death of Jina Mahsa Amini, a Kurdish-Iranian woman. Amini was brutally beaten by the police and died of cerebral hemorrhaging. Since then, the slogan "Woman, Life, Freedom" has been heard incessantly in Iran and echoed around the globe. In her honor and for all those fighting for civil liberties and freedom from fear, this issue features the translation of Iranian poet Ahmad Shamlou's "In the Square" by the Italian-Iranian scholar and writer Maziyar Ghiabi. Shamlou was an Iranian writer who wrote in Persian, not Arabic, but the thematic concerns of this poem echo the universal call for freedom in the region. There will undoubtedly be new, inspiring, and devastating developments long after these pages are in print, and poetry will keep voicing people's desire to live, our sense of justice, resistance to abuse, and the tragedy of our human condition.

Suja Sawafta, University of Miami
June 2023

ARABIC
إرادة الحياة
أبو القاسم الشابي

إذا الشَّعْبُ يومًا أرادَ الحياةَ
فلا بُدَّ أنْ يَسْتجيبَ القدرْ
ولا بُدَّ لِلَّيْلِ أنْ ينجلي
ولا بُدَّ للقيدِ أن يَنْكَسِرْ
ومَن لم يعانِقْهُ شَوقُ الحياةِ
تَبَخَّرَ في جَوِّها واندَثَرْ
فويلٌ لِمَنْ لم تَشُقْهُ الحياةُ
من صَفْعَةِ العَدَمِ المنتصِرْ
كذلك قالتْ ليَ الكائناتُ
وحدَّثَني روحُها المُسْتَتِرْ
ودَمْدَمَتِ الرِّيحُ بَيْنَ الفِجاجِ
وفوقَ الجبالِ وتحتَ الشَّجَرْ
إذا مَا طَمحْتُ إلى غايةٍ
رَكِبْتُ المنى ونَسِيتُ الحَذَرْ
ولم أتجنَّبْ وُعورَ الشِّعابِ
ولا كُبَّةَ اللَّهَبِ المُسْتَعِرْ
ومن لا يحبُّ صُعودَ الجبالِ
يَعِشْ أبَدَ الدَّهرِ بَيْنَ الحُفَرْ
فَعَجَّتْ بقلبي دماءُ الشَّبابِ
وضجَّت بصدري رياحٌ أخَرْ
وأطرقتُ أصغي لقصفِ الرُّعودِ
وعزفِ الرِّياحِ وَوَقْعِ المَطَرْ
وقالتْ ليَ الأرضُ لما سألتُ

أيا أمُّ هل تكرهينَ البَشَرْ
أباركُ في النَّاسِ أهلَ الطُموحِ
ومَن يَسْتَلِذُّ ركوبَ الخطرْ
وألعنُ مَنْ لا يماشي الزَّمانَ
ويقنعُ بالعيشِ عيشِ الحجرْ
هو الكونُ حيٌّ يحبُّ الحَيَاةَ

***

ولولا أُمومَةُ قلبي الرَّؤومُ لمَا
ضمَّتِ الميْتَ تِلْكَ الحُفَرْ
فويلٌ لمنْ لم تَشُقْهُ الحَيَاةُ
مِنْ لعنةِ العَدَمِ المنتصرْ

فلا بُدَّ أنْ يَسْتَجيبَ القدرْ
ولا بُدَّ للَّيْلِ أنْ ينجلي
ولا بُدَّ للقيدِ أن يَنْكَسِرْ

Abul Qassem al-Shabbi was a Tunisian poet. He is best known for writing the final two verses of the Tunisian National Anthem. His famous poem "The Will of Life" was considered the anthem of the revolutions of the Arab Spring, which began in late 2010 and early 2011 and ended in 2013. He died in 1934 at the age of 25.

The Will to Life (redacted)

Translated by Suja Sawafta

If one day the people will to live
Then fate has no choice but to comply
The darkness of the night will dissipate
The chains will break and give way
He who does not embrace the longing of life
Will evaporate into thin air and fade away
For the one that life does not burden
Will never face victory in a state of nothingness
This is what the beings told me
Thus spoke their hidden spirits
The wind's murmur was heard between the fractures
Over the mountains and under the trees:
If I do not aspire to a goal,
Pursue the object of my desire without prudence
Neither the rugged canyons will I evade
Nor the rage of a blazing fire
He who doesn't climb mountains
Will forever remain in hollows
The blood of youth rushes through my heart
And a wind blasts through my chest
So I listened to the raging thunders
The call of the wind and the fall of the rain
And the Earth said to me—when I turned to her and asked,
"Mother Earth, do you hate humankind?

To which she answered:
"Among you all, I bless the ambitious
Who enjoy taking risks and
Curse those who pay no mind to time,
Those who despise the dead, no matter how great they are
The horizon does not embrace dead birds
And the bees do not glide to dead flowers.

I curse those who lead a life, stagnant like stone.
The universe is alive and it loves life
Were it not for the maternal nature of my heart's tenderness
Its graves would not have held the dead
For the one that life does not burden
Will never face victory in a state of nothingness

If one day the people will to live
Then fate has no choice but to comply
The darkness of the night will dissipate
The chains will break and give way

Suja Sawafta is Palestinian-American critic and writer. Her writing has appeared in *The Baffler, Vogue Arabia, The Emancipator/ Boston Globe, Grazia Middle East, Arab Lit Quarterly, Middle East Monitor,* and *Words Without Borders.* She is assistant professor and director of Arabic studies at the University of Miami. She is currently at work on her first book on Abdulrahman Munif, a Saudi-Iraqi petroleum economist turned novelist.

ليس نجمًا

أدونيس

ليس نجمًا ليس إيحاءَ نبيٍّ
ليس وجهًا خاشعًا للقمرِـ

هوذا يأتي كرمحٍ وثنيّ
غازيًا أرضَ الحروفْ
نازفًاـ يرفع للشمس نزيفهْ؛

هوذا يلبس عُرْيَ الحجَرِ
ويصلّي للكهوفْ؛

هوذا يحتضنُ الأرضَ الخفيفة.

No Star

Translated by Kareem James Abu-Zeid and Ivan S. Eubanks

No star, no prophet's inspiration,
No face submissive to the moon—

He is at hand, a pagan spear
Invading the land of letters,
Bleeding, lifting his blood to the sun,

Adorned in naked stone,
Praying to caverns,

He embraces the weightless world.

آخر السّماء

يحْلم أن يرميَ عينيه في
قرارة المدينة الآتيةُ
يحلم أن يرقص في الهاويه
يَحْلم أن يجهلَ أيّامه الآكلةَ الأشياءْ
أيّامه الخالقةَ الأشياءْ؛

يحلم أن ينهضَ أن يَنْهارْ
كالبحرِ ـ أن يسْتعجلَ الأسرار
مُبتدِئاً سماءَه في آخر السماءْ.

The Sky's End

He dreams he casts his eyes
To the depths of the coming city,
He dreams he dances in the abyss,
He dreams he knows no days
Of hunger or creation.

He dreams he swells and breaks
Like the sea—he dreams he impels the secrets
And sets his sky in motion
At the sky's end.

شدّاد

عاد شَدّادُ عادْ
فَارْفعوا راية الحنينْ
واتْركوا رفضكم إشارهْ
في طريق السّنينْ
فوق هذي الحجارهْ،
بِاسْم ذات العمادْ.

إنّها وطَنُ الرّافضينْ
أَلّذين يسوقون أعمارَهم يائسينْ
كسَروا خاتَمَ القَماقِمِ
واسْتَهزأوا بالوعيدْ
بجسور السّلامهْ،

إنّها أرضُنا وميراثُنا الوحيدْ
نحنُ أبناءَها المُنظَرينَ ليوم القيامَهْ.

Shaddad

Shaddad has returned,
So raise the banner of longing,
Leave your refusal behind, a sign
On these stones
In the path of years—
Do this in the name of the city of pillars.

It is the home of rebels
Who lead their desperate lives,
Who broke the amphorae's seals,
Who laugh at threats
And the bridges of peace.

It is our land and only heritage,
We are its sons awaiting
The day of judgment and resurrection.

مرثية الحلّاج

ريشتُك المسمومة الخضراءْ
ريشتُك المنفوخةُ الأوداج باللّهيبْ
بالكوكب الطّالع من بغدادْ
تاريخُنا وبعثنا القريبْ
في أرضنا ـ في موتِنا المُعادْ.

ألزّمنُ اسْتلقى على يديكْ
والنّارُ في عينيكْ
مجتاحةٌ تمتدُّ للسماءْ

يا كوكباً يطلعُ من بغدادْ
مُحَمَّلاً بالشعر والميلادْ،
يا ريشةً مسمومةً خضراءْ.

لم يبقَ للآتينَ من بعيدْ
مع الصّدى والموتِ والجليدْ
في هذه الأرض النُّشوريّةْـ
لم يبقَ إلّا أنتَ والحضورْ
يا لُغة الرَّعدِ الجليليّةْ
في هذه الأرض القُشوريّةْ
يا شاعرا الأسرارِ والجذورْ.

Adonis is a Syrian poet, essayist, and translator. He led a modernist revolution in the second half of the 20th century, "exerting seismic influence" on Arabic poetry by incorporating modernist approaches to free verse.

Elegy for al-Hallaj

Your poisonous green plume,
Your plume whose veins swell with flames,
Raging like the star rising from Baghdad,
Is our history and coming resurrection
In our land—in our death reborn.

Time lies in your hands
And the raging fire in your eyes
Spreads to the heavens,
Star rising from Baghdad,
Laden with poetry and birth,
Poisonous green plume.

Kareem James Abu-Zeid is an award-winning freelance translator of authors from across the Arab world. His most recent translations are Najwan Darwish's *Exhausted on the Cross,* winner of the 2022 Sarah Maguire Prize, and Olivia Elias' *Chaos, Crossing*. He lives in the countryside just outside of Santa Fe, New Mexico. He is also the author of the book *The Poetics of Adonis and Yves Bonnefoy: Poetry as Spiritual Practice* (2021). The online hub for his work is www.kareemjamesabuzeid.com.

Ivan S. Eubanks translates poetry and prose and conducts research in comparative literature and literary history. He has a Ph.D. in Slavic Languages from Princeton University. He is also a filmmaker and is currently Dean of Business and Finance at the University College of the Cayman Islands.

Nothing remains in this land of resurrection
For those coming from afar
With echoes, ice, and death—
Nothing remains in this flayed land
But you and presence,
Galilean tongue of thunder,
Poet of secrets and roots.

"No Star", "The Sky's End", "Shaddad", and "Elegy for al-Hallaj", by Adonis, translated by Kareem James Abu-Zeid, from Songs of Mihyar the Damascene, copyright ©1961, 1970, 1988 by Adonis. Translation copyright ©2019 by Kareem James Abu-Zeid and Ivan Eubanks. Reprinted by permission of New Directions Publishing Corp.

From *Songs of Mihyar the Damascene* by Adonis published by Penguin Classics. Copyright © Adonis, 1961, 1970, 1988, 1996. Translation copyright © Kareem James Abu-Zeid and Ivan Eubanks, 2019. Reprinted by permission of Penguin Books Limited.

تونسيّ، دُفعةً واحدةً، أو لا أكونْ

محمد الصغير أولاد احمد

بحياتي نِلْتُ ما تسمُو بهِ هذي الحياةْ
وزرعتُ الشكَّ في أرضِ اليقينْ
تونسيٌ مرّةً واحدةً
تونسيٌ دُفعةً واحدةً.. أوْ لا أكونْ

لامَني الصمتُ على صمتي الطويلْ
وعلى خوفي من الخوفِ العليلْ
لم أكنْ وحدي أنادي:
"ارحلوا الآنَ وفورًا...ارحلوا الآنَ"
فكانوا يرحلونْ ..
تونسيٌّ مرّةً واحدةً
تونسيٌّ دُفعةً واحدةً أوْ لا أكونْ

أكتبُ الآنَ نشيدي بدمي
لشهيدٍ كان صوتي وفمي
لغدٍ لم يأتني يا صاحبي منذ قرونْ
تونسيٌّ مرّةً واحدةً
تونسيٌّ، دُفعةً واحدةً، أو لا أكونْ

لم تكنْ لي ذكرياتٌ معهمْ
لم تعدْ لي ذكرياتٌ معهمْ
لا فراشاتٍ ولا حقلَ

(ولا قالَ ولا زارَ ولا يحيا ولا ماتَ)
ولا هم يحزنونْ
تونسيٌّ مرّةً واحدةً
تونسيٌّ دُفعةً واحدةً.. أوْ لا أكونْ

ليس لي وقتٌ لوقتٍ سابقٍ
ليس لي وقتٌ لوقتٍ لاحقٍ
اكتبُ الآنَ وأنتم تبدِعون
تونسيٌّ مرّةً واحدةً
تونسيٌّ دُفعةً واحدةً.. حدَّ الجنونْ

لم أطُل من كوكبِ الدنيا سوى نجمَ الحياةْ
ولأني عربيّ.. فرّ منّي وهربْ
مُشعلاً أرضَ العربْ
أيّ نورٍ، بعد هذا، تبتغُونْ؟
تونسيّ مرةً واحدةً
تونسيّ دفعةً واحدةً.. أو لا أكونْ

لم أجدْ صوتاً يُغني لي قصيدي
كلهمْ غنّوا إلى العهد البليدِ
واستمرّوا، بعد هذا، يمدحونْ
تونسيٌّ مرّةً واحدةً
تونسيٌّ دُفعةً واحدةً.. أوْ لا أكونْ

(١٦ مارس ٢٠١١)

Tunisian I am, for once and for all, or else I will not be

Translated by Hanan Natour

By my life, I have achieved what life has strived for
I sowed the seeds of doubt in the soil of certitude.
Tunisian, all at once,
Tunisian, for once and for all…or else I will not be.

Silence had been blaming me for my own silence
and for my fear of the sick, ailing fear.
I was not alone when I called out:
"Leave now, immediately…Leave now"
So they left.
Tunisian, all at once,
Tunisian, for once and for all…or else I will not be.

Now I write my own anthem with my own blood
for a martyr who was my voice and mouth
for a tomorrow which never came for centuries, dear friend.
Tunisian, all at once,
Tunisian, for once and for all…or else I will not be.

I did not have any memories with them
I no longer have any memories with them.
No butterflies nor fields
(and nor did he speak nor visit nor live nor die)
And nor did they mourn.
Tunisian, all at once,
Tunisian, for once and for all…or else I will not be.

I have no time for a time which has passed
I have no time for a time which is to come
I am now writing while you are all creating and inventing.
Tunisian, all at once,

Tunisian, for once and for all…to the edge of madness.

All that I could ever see from the planet of this world, was the star of life
And as I am Arab…it escaped from me and fled
Setting aflame the land of the Arabs.
Which other light after all this, are you all wishing for?
Tunisian, all at once,
Tunisian, for once and for all…or else I will not be.

I could not find a voice to sing to me my poem
All of them were singing for a dull, spiritless era
and they are still continuing after all this to give praise to it.
Tunisian, all at once,
Tunisian I am, for once and for all…or else I will not be.

March 16th, 2011

مصعدٌ باتّجاهِ الهاوية

السابع من نوفمبر ١٩٨٧

طلعَ الجيشُ علينا
ببيانٍ مدنيْ
فغدرْنا بنبي
وغُدِرْنا بنبيْ
أيها المبعوثُ فينا:
انّه وقْعُ حذاءٍ عسكريْ!!

الثالث والعشرون من أكتوبر ٢٠١١

طلعَ الجهلُ علينا
ببيانٍ فِئويْ
فغدرْنا بجَبانٍ
وغُدِرْنا بتقيْ
أيها المبعوثُ فينا:
انهُ وقْعُ ريالٍ قطريْ!!

التاسع من أفريل ٢٠١٢

طلعَ الحقدُ علينا
بكلامٍ أُخْرَوِيْ
فاستجابتْ شرطةُ الحيِّ..بقصفٍ نَوَوِيْ
أيها المبعوثُ فينا:
ارْحلِ الآن..وعشْ كالمُنْزَوِيْ!!

....

في انتظار غرّة ماي ٢٠١٢

(١١ نوفيمبر ٢٠١١)

Muhammad al-Saghir Awlad Ahmad was one of Tunisia's most acclaimed poets and one of few Tunisian writers who stood in a mutual literary dialogue with other Arab writers such as the celebrated Palestinian poet Mahmoud Darwish. Awlad Ahmad acted as a figure of resistance and protest poetry since the 1970s, lending his voice both to the "bread riots" in 1984 and to the Tunisian uprisings of 2010 and 2011. His collection devoted to the most recent uprisings is titled *Al-Qiyada al-Shi'riyya li-l-Thawra al-Tunisiyya* (2013) (*The Poetic Leadership of the Tunisian Revolution*). Beyond his poetry of protest, he is known as the founder of the Tunisian *Bayt al-Shi'r* (*House of Poetry*), which continues to be a center of performed poetry in the heart of the capital city's medina.

Ascending towards the Abyss

November 7th 1987
The army loomed over us
With a civilian announcement
So we deceived with a prophet
And were deceived by a prophet:
Oh you who were sent as a messenger among us
That is the heavy step of a military boot!

October 23rd 2011
Ignorance loomed over us
With a factional announcement
So we deceived with a coward
And were deceived by a pious believer:
Oh you who were sent as a messenger among us
That is the jingle of a Qatari Riyal!

Hanan Natour is a doctoral researcher of Tunisian literature at Freie Universität Berlin and served as a research associate at the ERC-funded project "PalREAD – Country of Words: Reading and Reception of Palestinian Literature from 1948 to the Present" (2019–2023). She holds an MPhil in Modern Middle Eastern Studies from the University of Oxford and a BA in both Arabic Studies and German Literature from the University of Göttingen including one year of study at the Sorbonne.

April 9th 2012
Hatred loomed over us
With the words of the ethereal realm
So the local police responded…with a nuclear strike
Oh you who were sent as a messenger among us:
Leave now…and live like a hermit and recluse!

…
Waiting for May 2012 to begin.

(11th November 2011)

Translator's note: A note of thanks goes to Professor Mohamed-Salah Omri, Dr. Ruth Abou Rached, and Calum Humphreys who kindly shared their thoughts on these translations with me. "Ascending towards the Abyss" is based on the famous nasheed "Tala'u al-badr alayana".

ثورة على الشّمس
نازك الملائكة

هدية إلى المتمردين

وَقَفَتْ أمام الشمس صارخةً بها
يا شمسُ، مثلُكِ قلبيَ المتمرِّدُ
قلبي الذي جَرَفَ الحياةَ شبابُه
وَسَقَى النجومَ ضياؤه المتجدِّدُ
مهلاً، ولا يخدعْكِ حُزنٌ حائرٌ
في مقلتيَّ، ودَمعةٌ تتنهّدُ

فالحزنُ صورةُ ثورتي وتمرُّدي
تحت الليالي والألوهةُ تَشهدُ
مَهلاً ولا يخدَعكِ حزنُ ملامحي
وشحوبُ لوني وارتعاشُ عواطفي
وإذا لمحتِ على جبيني حَيْرتي
وسُطورَ حزني الشاعريِّ الجارفِ
فهو الشعورُ يُثيرُ في نفسي الأسى
والدمعَ في هول الحياة العاصفِ
وهي النبوّةُ لم تطرْ فتمرّدَتْ
بالحُزْنِ في وجهِ الحياةِ الكاسفِ

شَفَتايَ مُطبَقتان فوق أساهما
عينايَ ظامئتانِ للأنداءِ
تَرَكَ المساءُ على جبيني ظلَّهُ
وقضى الصباحُ على جديدِ رجائي
فأتيتُ أسكُبُ في الطبيعة حَيْرتي
بين الشَّذَى والوردِ والأفياءِ

فسَخِرْتِ من حُزني العميقِ وأدمُعي
وَضحِكتِ فوق مرارتي وشَقائي

يا شمسُ! حتى أنتِ؟ يا لَكَآبتي
أنتِ التي ترنو لها أحلامي
أنتِ التي غنّى شَبَابي باسمها
وشَدَا بفيضِ ضيائِها البسَّام
أنتِ التي قدَّستُها وتَخذتُها
صَنَماً ألوذُ به من الآلام
يا خيبةَ الأحلامِ، ما أبقَيْتِ لي
إلا ظلالَ كآبتي وظلامي

سأحطِّمُ الصنَمَ الذي شيَّدْتُهُ
لكِ من هَوَايَ لكلِّ ضوءٍ ساطِعِ
وأُديرُ عينيْ عن سَناكِ مُشيحةً
ما أنتِ إلَّا طيفُ ضوءٍ خادِعِ
وأصوغ من أحلامِ قلبي جَنَّةً
تُغْني حياتي عن سَناكِ اللَّامع
نحنُ، الخياليِّينَ، في أرواحنا
سرُّ الألوهةِ والخُلودِ الضائع

لا تَنْشُري الأضواءَ فوق خميلتي
إنْ تُشرقي، فلغيرِ قلبي الشاعر
ما عاد ضوؤكِ يستثيرُ خوالجي
حَسْبي نجومُ الليلِ تُلهِمُ خاطري
هنَّ الصديقاتُ السواهرُ في الدُّجَى
يفهمن روحي وانفجارَ مشاعري
ويُرِقْنَ في جَفْني خُيوطَ أشعَّةٍ
فِضيَّةٍ، تحتَ المساءِ الساحر

الليلُ ألحانُ الحياة وشِعْرُها
ومَطَافُ آلهةِ الجَمالِ المُلهِمِ
تهفو عليه النفسُ غيرَ حبيسةٍ
وتحلِّق الأرواحُ فوقَ الأنْجُمِ
كم سِرْتُ تحتَ ظَلامه ونجومِهِ
فنسِيتُ أحزانَ الوجودِ المُظْلِمِ
وعلى فمي نَغَمٌ إلهيُّ الصَدى
تُلْقِيهِ قافلةُ النجومِ على فمي

كم رُحْتُ أرقبُ كلَّ نجمٍ عابرٍ
وأصوغُ في غَسَقِ الظلامِ ملاحني
أو أرقبُ القَمَرَ المودَّعَ في الدجى
وأهيمُ في وادي الخيالِ الفاتنِ
الصمتُ يبعَثُ في فؤادي رعشةً
تحت المساءِ المُذْلَهِمِّ الساكنِ
والضوءُ يرقصُ في جفوني راسماً
في عُمقِها أحلامَ قلبٍ آمنِ

يا شمسُ، أمّا أنتِ.. ماذا؟ ما الذي
تلقاهُ فيكِ عواطفي وخواطري؟
لا تَعْجَبي إن كنتُ عاشقةَ الدجى
يا ربَّةَ اللَّهبِ المذيبِ الصاهرِ
يا من تُمَزِّقُ كلَّ حُلْمٍ مُشرقٍ
للحالمينَ وكلَّ طيفٍ ساحرِ
يا من تُهدِّمُ ما يشيِّدُهُ الدُجى
والصمْتُ في أعماقِ قلبِ الشاعرِ

أضواؤكِ المتراقصاتُ جميعُها
يا شمسُ أضعفُ من لهيبِ تمرُّدي

وجنونُ نارِكِ لن يمزِّقَ نغمتي
ما دام قيثاري المغرِّدُ في يدي
فإذا غَمَرْتِ الأرضَ فَلْتَتَذَكَّري
أني سأخلي من ضيائكِ مَعْبدي
وسأدفِنُ الماضيْ الذي جَلَّلتِه
ليخيِّمَ الليلُ الجميلُ على غَدي

Revolt Against the Sun

Translated by Emily Drumsta

A gift to the rebels.

She stood before the sun, screaming out loud:
Oh Sun, my rebel's heart is just like you:
while young, it washed away much of my life,
its lights quenched the stars' thirst, ever renewed.
Careful – don't let the sadness in my eyes
or these copious tears deceive your sight.
This sadness is the form of my revolt,
to which the gods bear witness every night.

Careful, don't be deceived by my pale skin,
these quivering emotions, this dark frown.
If you see indecision, or the lines
of fierce poetic sadness on my brow,
know that it's feeling causing my soul's grief
and tears at life's terror – it's prophecy
that failed to fly, but stood up to resist
a life of sadness and melancholy.

My lips are fastened shut over their pain,
my eyes are thirsty for sweet drops of dew,
the evening left its shadow on my brow
and morning's killed off all my pleas to you.
I came to pour out my uncertainty
in nature, amid fragrances and shade,
but you, Sun, mocked my sadness and my tears
and laughed, from up above, at all my pain.

Even you, Sun? Alas, what misery!
You were the one I yearned for in my dreams,
you were the one whose name I once revered,

singing the praises of your smiling beams.
You were the one I once held sacred and
idolized as a refuge from all pain.
But now, crusher of dreams, melancholy,
darkness, and shadows are all that remain.

I will shatter the idol that I built
to you out of my love for radiance
and turn my eyes away from your bright light –
you're nothing but a ghost, splendor's pretense.
I'll build a heaven out of hidden hopes
And live without your luminosity.
We dreamers know we hold within our souls
divine secrets, a lost eternity.

Do not spread out your beams over my grove,
You rise for other than my poet's heart.
Your light no longer stirs feelings in me,
the night stars now inspire all my art.
They are the friends who guard me in the dark,
they understand the feelings that ignite
my spirit, they extend thin, silver threads
to guide my eyes through the enchanted night.

Night is life's melody, its poetry,
here gods of beauty roam to their content,
here uninhibited souls fly about
and spirits hover in the firmament.
How often I have wandered to forget
life's gloomy sorrows in the evening's dark,
upon my lips, a divine melody
recited by a caravan of stars.

How often I have watched stars as they pass
letting the twilight tune my incantations,
and watched the moon bidding the night goodbye,
and roamed the valleys of imagination.

The silence sends a shiver through my spine
beneath the evening's dome, so still and dark,
light dances, painting on my eyelids with
the dreamy palette of a peaceful heart.

And as for you, oh Sun… what can I say?
What can my feelings hope to find in you?
Don't be surprised that I'm in love with night,
goddess of cruel flames that melt us through.
You rend our dreams on the horizon line,
you decimate what we build in the dark,
you shatter magic visions, ghostly dreams,
and break the silence in a poet's heart.

All of your dancing lights look pale, oh Sun,
compared to my resistance and its fire.
Your mad flames can't tear up my melody
so long as my hands grasp this singing lyre.
And when you flood the earth, remember this:
My temple has no room for your cruel light
I aim to bury the past you revealed
And live beneath the canopy of night.

July 8th, 1946

أغنية للقمر

كَأسُ حليبٍ مُثلّجٍ تَرِفِ / أم جدولٌ سائلٌ من الصَّدَفِ؟
أم غَسَقٌ أبيضٌ يسيلُ / خدود ليلٍ مُعَطَّرِ السُّدُفِ
أم حُقّ عطرٍ ملوَّنٍ خَضِلٍ / يقطُرُ شهداً لكلّ مُغترِفِ؟
أم أنتَ خَدٌّ مُزَنبقٌ أرِجٌ / يَنعَسُ فوق الأعشابِ والسَعَفِ؟
ما أنتَ يا دورقَ الضياءِ ويا / كواكباً في الظلام مُنْصَهِره؟

يا قُبَلاً سَوسنيَّةً سَكَبَتْ / شهداً مُصفّىً في ليلةٍ عَطِرَهْ
يا مَخبأً للجمالِ يا حُزَماً / من زنبقٍ في السماء مُنْعَصِرَهْ
ويا شِفاهاً من الضياءِ دَنَتْ / تَمسَحُ وجهة العرائشِ النَضِرَهْ
يا بركةَ العِطرِ والنعومةِ يا / سلَّةَ فُلٍّ في الأُفْقِ منحدِره

يا زورقَ العاشقين تحمِلُهُم / عبْرَ بحار الأحلامِ والكَسَلِ
على جَناحٍ مريَّشٍ يقظٍ / يفرُشُ دربَ الغرامِ بالأملِ
يا منبعاً يسكُبُ النُّعاسَ على / ما أرَّقَتْهُ الأشواقُ من مُقَلِ
يا ساقيَ الأعينِ الرقاقِ رؤىً / يا كوبَ نومٍ مخدِّرٍ ثَمِلِ
يا أصبعاً يلمُسُ الجراحَ ويا / مُبَعْثَرَ الأُغْنياتِ والقُبَلِ

جزيرةٌ في الدُّجَى معلَّقةٌ / فجريَّةُ اللونِ والتباشيرِ
طافيةٌ فوق جدولٍ عبِقٍ / مكوكبُ الشاطئَينِ مَسحورِ
تجمَّدَ الضوءُ عند شاطئها / مهدُ حريرٍ وكَنْزَ بلّورِ
يا توبةَ القُبْحِ يا شِراعَ هوىً / مُلَوَّنٍ ناعمِ الأساريرِ
يا نَدَمَ الليلِ والظلام ويا / كفّارةَ الغَيْمِ والأعاصيرِ

أذِبْ شظايا أشعَّةٍ ورؤىً / في الليلِ واغمُرْ سُطوحَنا فِضَّهْ
وانفُضْ جناحيكَ في الفضاءِ يَسِلْ / لونُ جناحِ الفراشةِ الغَضَّهْ
لولاكَ لم تَرقُصِ الظلالُ ولم / تبرُدْ كؤوسُ الزنابقِ البَضَّهْ
غزلْتَ أحلامَنا وأرضعْنا / ضياؤكَ العذبُ ومضةً ومضَّهْ

يا كوَّةَ الفَجْرِ في دُجَىً تَعِبِ يا مُطْعِمَ الياسمينِ في الرَوْضه
البَثْ كما أنتَ عالماً عجِزَتْ أرواحُنا أنْ تعيْ خفاياهُ
يا ناسِجَ الشِعرِ يا بَقيَّتَهُ في عالمٍ أظْلَمَتْ مَراياهُ
أيُّ نشيدٍ لم ينبجِس عَسَلاً وأنتَ تفترّ في ثناياهُ
زِنتَ مِنحَتَ الغناءَ لذَّتَهُ يا نبْضَةَ الوزنِ في حناياهُ
فابْق وراءَ الحياةِ أخيلةً الشِعرُ فيها والحُبّ واللهُ

(١٩٥٢)

Nazik al-Mala'ika was an Iraqi poet born in Baghdad. She was among the country's greatest writers and was best known for being among the first Arab poets to use free verse. She died in Cairo in 2007.

A Song for the Moon

Sumptuous glass of chilly milk or flowing stream of pearl?
White twilight painted on the cheeks of a sweet-smelling night?
A colored jar of musk dripping honey with every scoop?
Or fragrant, lily-white cheeks sleeping on cool, dewy grass?

What are you, carafe leaking light, stars melting into dark?
Lily-of-valley kisses, honey poured in pitch-black night?
Refuge of beauty, bundled blooms clutched in the sky's soft hands?
Lips made of light come down to kiss the verdant face of land?
A lake of supple jasmine poured out from the firmament?

You are the lovers' boat; you carry them on languid seas,
on feathered, wakeful wings that spread the path of love with hope.
You are a spring pouring out sleep on eyelids soft with cares,
a cupbearer for dreaming eyes, a glass of druggy sleep.
You are a finger scattering songs, a hand caressing wounds,

an island hung in darkness, its color presaging dawn,
floating above a fragrant stream with magic, starlit banks,
light frozen on its muddy edge, silk cradle, crystal trove.
You're shame's repentance and love's sail, colorful and
soft-featured, you're night's regret,
you make amends for tornadoes and clouds.

Melt bits of beams and dreams in night and drown our roofs in silver,
shake off your wings in skies stained with color like butterflies.
Without you, shadows would not dance, the irises' tender cups
could not be chilled. you wooed our dreams and nursed us,
beam by beam.

Small aperture of dawn inside a darkness of fatigue,
stay as you are, a secret world our souls can't comprehend,
weaver of poetry's remnants in worlds of darkened mirrors.

You make each song mellifluous by shimmering in its folds,
you give music its flavor, pulsing meter through its curves.
Stay as the fantasies sustaining life – love, poems, God.

1952

Emily Drumsta is assistant professor of Middle Eastern Studies and French & Italian Studies at the University of Texas at Austin. Her forthcoming book, *Ways of Seeking*, explores the history of detection and investigation in twentieth-century Arabic fiction. Her translation, *Revolt Against the Sun: The Selected Poetry of Nazik al-Mala'ika* (Saqi Books in 2020), was the recipient of a PEN/Heim Translation prize in 2018. Her next book project, tentatively titled *Good Measure: Poetic Form, Popular Politics, and Questions of Meter in Modern Arabic Poetry*, has been funded by a 2022 NEH Summer Stipend. She is a co-founder of Tahrir Documents, an online archive of newspapers, broadsides, pamphlets, and other ephemera collected in Cairo's Tahrir Square during the 2011 uprisings in Egypt.

Selections from Revolt Against the Sun by Nazik al-Mala'ika translated by Emily Drumsta, Translation copyright ©2020 by Emily Drumsta. Reprinted by permission of Saqi Books.

كلبةٌ ضالّةٌ

فرح برقاوي

لا بيتَ لي
أجوبُ شوارعَ المدينة

حين تزرقُّ السماءُ، تُحبّني
وتَسكنني الأرضُ
حين أراقبُ الغيوم

أصابعٌ خفيّةٌ تمسّدُ
وبري المبلّلَ من
صقيعِ الصمت

أنظرُ للعابرين
وهم ينظرون إليّ
ينثرون الفُتاتَ أمامي
لكنّ بقايا الأطعمةِ جميعها
لا تُشبعني

لا نُباحَ لي
ولا اسمًا ولا عنوانًا يُطوّقُ رقبتي
أمشيْ وأمشيْ
أعاودُ الدورانَ في نفسِ الشوارعِ
علّي أحتَطني عليها
أو أحتّطها بداخلي

أُقلّدُ الأصواتَ حَولي
لأُشبِهها:
ضَحكاتُ طفلةٍ تُجرّبُ المشي
حديثٌ صباحيٌّ بينَ جارتين تشكوان جارتَهُما الثالثة
ارتشافُ القهوةِ بينَ شفتيّ عجوزٍ شاردٍ اتّخذَ
من مقعدٍ على الرصيفِ مقهاهُ المفضّل
تسلّلُ الساعي من الأبوابِ إلى صناديقِ البريد
وقضمُ عجلاتِ الدرّاجة لأوراقِ الخريف

أُقلّدُ الأصواتَ
تَصيرُ عائلتي
وأصيرُ أنا،
برغمِ ضلالي،
ابنتَها المفضّلة

كلبةٌ ضالّةٌ
صدري مُدَلدَلٌ كفاكهةٍ
جاهزةٍ للقطف
بعد أن أشبَعتُ الكثيرَ من الأفواه
تَنِزّ جروحي كلَّ ليلةٍ
بعدَ مشيٍ طويل
يبتلُّ وَبري مهما نشّفَتهُ الشمسُ
فألعَقُني برفق
أكتبُ شعرًا لأجلِ نُدوبي
وأعودُ إلى دورِ البطولة
عندما يأتي الصباح

Stray

Translated by Katharine Halls

No home to go to
I roam the city streets

The sky loves me when it's blue
and the ground makes its home
in me when I
watch the clouds above

Invisible fingers kneading
my fur damp
with silence frost

I watch passersby
as they watch me
and scatter crumbs
but all these leftovers
do not satisfy

I have no bark
no name or address to collar my neck
I walk and walk
in circles through the same streets
mummifying myself in them perhaps
or them inside of me

I imitate the voices to
make them mine:
a little girl learning to walk
morning conversation, two neighbors
complaining about a third
coffee on the lips of an old man lost in thought, a seat on the
pavement his favorite café

postman slipping from door to mailbox
bike wheels eating autumn leaves

I imitate the voices
they become my family
and I become,
though I am lost,
the daughter they love best

Stray dog
nipples dangle like ripe fruit
after feeding many
wounds bleed at night
from walking so far
fur wet even in the brightest sun
I lick myself tenderly
write poetry for my scars
take the lead again
when morning comes

سؤال العودة

كيف يعودُ الناسُ من الحرب؟
كيف يعودون
من النيران؟ من الأغلال؟
من الأعضاءِ المبتورة؟
من بطنِ الحوتِ الجائع؟
كيف يعودون؟

***

كيف يعودُ الناسُ من القهر؟
من العتمة؟
من الأحلامِ المسروقةِ
إلى الأحلامِ،
كيف يعودون؟

***

كيف يعودون من الخوفِ
من الموتِ
من الفقدِ
إلى الخوفِ من الحياة؟
إلى الحياةِ،
كيف يعودون؟

***

كيف يعودون من الشِّعر؟
من الحب؟
من الهزيمة في الحب؟
إلى هزيمةٍ أخرى،
ثمَّ إلى حضنِ الحب
ثانيةً
كيف يعودون؟

***

كيف يعود الناسُ من الإلحادِ إلى الإيمان؟
كيف يعودون من العجلاتِ إلى الخطوات؟
كيف يعودون من الأقبيةِ إلى الشطآن؟
كيف يعودون من الخَرَسِ إلى الكلمات؟
كيف يعودون من الأبنيةِ إلى الساحات؟

ومن ثمّ،
كيف يعودُ الناسُ من النورِ إلى الإنكار؟
كيف يعودون من الفنِّ إلى جشعِ الإنتاج؟
كيف يعودون من العِلمِ إلى شاشاتِ الإعلام؟

وحقًّا كيف؟
بعدَ كُلّ هذا،
كيف يعودون
إلى أنفُسِهم؟

***

كَ
يْ
فَ

يعودون؟

Farah Barqawi is a Palestinian writer, poet, performer, educator, and feminist organizer. Her work has been featured in multiple languages on prominent online platforms such as Michigan Quarterly Review, Mada Masr, Al-Jumhuriya, and Jeem, and in multiple anthologies, such as *Ce que la Palestine apporte au monde* (IMA, France, 2023) and *We Wrote in Symbols* (Saqi Books, UK, 2021). In 2019, she produced and hosted a season of the Arabic podcast Eib (Taboo). She wrote and directed the solo theatre piece "Baba, Come to Me," which she has performed in several cities around the world. She is the co-founder of two feminist projects: Wiki Gender and The Uprising of Women in the Arab World. Farah is an MFA candidate in non-fiction creative writing at New York University, where she also teaches creative writing to undergraduates.

The Question of Return

How do people return from war?
How do they return
from fires? from shackles and chains?
from severed limbs?
from the belly of the ravening whale?
How do they return?

How do people return from being broken?
from darkness?
From stolen dreams
to dreams,
how do they return?

How do they return from fear
of death
of loss
to fear of life?
To life,
how do they return?

How do they return from poetry?
from love?
From defeat in love
to another defeat,
then love's embrace
again
how do they return?

How do people return from unbelief to faith?
wheels to footsteps,
tunnels to riverbanks,

muteness to words,
buildings to open fields?

Then again, how is it
that people return from light to denial, how?
from art to the hunger to produce, how?
from insight to TV screens?

And how,
after everything
do they return
to themselves?

Katharine Halls is an Arabic-to-English translator from Cardiff, Wales. Her critically acclaimed translation of Ahmed Naji's prison memoir *Rotten Evidence* was a finalist for the National Book Critics Circle autobiography award, she was awarded a 2021 PEN/Heim Translation Fund Grant for her translation of Haytham El-Wardany's *Things That Can't Be Fixed* and her translation, with Adam Talib, of Raja Alem's *The Dove's Necklace* received the 2017 Sheikh Hamad Award for Translation. She is one third of teneleven, an agency for contemporary Arabic literature.

ارحل

رامي عصام

كلنا إيد واحدة
وطلبنا حاجة واحدة
ارحل ارحل ارحل ارحل

كلنا إيد واحدة
وطلبنا حاجة واحدة
ارحل ارحل ارحل ارحل

يسقط يسقط حسني مبارك
يسقط يسقط حسني مبارك

الشعب يريد إسقاط النظام
الشعب يريد إسقاط النظام
الشعب يريد إسقاط النظام
الشعب يريد إسقاط النظام

هو يمشي مش حنمشي
هو يمشي مش حنمشي

كلنا إيد واحدة
وطلبنا حاجة واحدة
ارحل ارحل ارحل ارحل

كلنا إيد واحدة
وطلبنا حاجة واحدة
ارحل ارحل ارحل ارحل

Ramy Essam is an Egyptian musician. He is best known for his appearances in Cairo's Tahrir Square during the Egyptian Revolution of 2011. He was considered the voice of the Egyptian Revolution. His Song "Irhal (Leave)" was among the most popular protest songs of the Egyptian Uprising. The lyrics are reprinted with permission from the artist.

Get Out

Translated by Suja Sawafta

We are all united as one
And our demand is one thing

Get out
Leave
Depart
Get out

We are all united as one
And our demand is one thing

Get out
Leave
Depart
Get out

Down with Hosni Mubarak
Long may he fall

Down with Hosni Mubarak
Long may he fall

He must leave
We won't be the ones to go

He must be the one to leave
We won't be the ones to go

We are all united as one
And our demand is one thing

Get out
Leave
Depart
Get out

شعر بلا عنوان
السيد محمد حسين فضل الله

يا ظِلالَ الإسلامِ دَرْبُ الأعاصيرِ طَويلٌ في رحلةِ الإنسان
لَنْ تَكفَّ الزوابعُ السُّودُ، لن تَهدأ في الأفْقِ ثورةُ البُرْكان
لَن يَمَلَّ المُقامرونَ فما زالَ على الدَّربِ مَوْعِدٌ للرِّهان
غَيرَ أنَّ الحياةَ لا تَتْرُكُ الشَّوطَ كَئيباً في مُلتَقى الإيمان

*

دَوْرُنا: أن نحَرِّك الصَّوتَ في الأفْقِ لِيَبْقى معلَّقاً في الفَضاءِ
باحثاً في المَدى عَنِ الأُذنِ الظَّمْأى إليهِ في لَهْفَةِ الإصْغَاءِ
عَنْ كِيانٍ يَعيشُ في قَلَقِ الحَيرةِ، بَحْثاً عَنْ فِكرَةِ عَصماءِ
عَنْ غَدٍ يَحْضُنُ الهُدى، إن تخلَّى حاضِرُ الجيلِ عَنْ نِداءِ السَّماءِ

Al-Sayyid Mohammad Hussayn Fadlallah was an influential *marja' taqlid* based in Lebanon. Born in Najaf in 1935, he recited his first poem about the occupation of Palestine at age twelve. He later contributed regularly to the Iraqi Da'wa Party's Journal before migrating to Lebanon in 1966. He rose to prominence in 1978 and became a prolific writer during the most destructive phases of the Lebanese Civil War throughout the 1980s and 1990s. He was considered a major influence within the Lebanese Shiite socio-political sphere and died in Beirut, Lebanon in 2010 at age 74.

Untitled Poetry of Al-Sayyid Mohammad Hussayn Fadlallah

Translated by Alexander Nachman

Oh, shadow of Islam, your path of cyclones is long
in the journey of humanity
The black squalls will not tire,
the erupting volcano on the horizon will not quiet
The gamblers will not quit betting as long as there remains
an opportunity to bet
For life does not bleakly abandon the course
at the crossroads of faith

*

Our role: to mobilize the voice on the horizon,
so it remains suspended in space
In search of the ear that is thirsty to hear it, longing to listen
For an entity that lives in the anxiety of confusion,
in search of an infallible idea
For a tomorrow that contains guidance, if our generation gives up
the call of the heavens

Alexander Nachman holds a doctorate in Middle Eastern History from the University of Oxford. His research appears in various academic journals including Modern Intellectual History, British Journal of Middle Eastern Studies, Sociology of Islam, and others. He is currently working on a book about Ayatollah Khomeini.

مختارات من "تقاطعات"
جودت فخر الدين

— 1 —

يدْعوكَ السهْلُ الممْتَدُّ،
إلى نظَرٍ يمتَدُّ،
فتنْتَصِبُ الشجَرهْ.
تدْعوكَ إلى نظَرٍ في ذاتِكَ،
حيث الأسْرارُ الأسْرارُ،
بلا قِدّيسينَ ولا سَحَرهْ.

— 2 —

دَعْ أفكارَكَ تجلسُ كالأشياءِ بقُرْبِكَ،
حتى لو كانت حائرةً، أو غائمةً.
فالأشياءُ كذلكَ،
حتى لو كنتَ تَراها واضحةً، أو ثابتةً.
صادِقْ أفكارَكَ،
وألْفْها،
حتى لو كانت ترْحَلُ، أو تتغيّرُ، أو تتلاشى.
فالأشياءُ كذلكَ،
مهْما مَكَثَتْ.
دَعْ أفكارَكَ تخرجُ من رأسِكَ،
تلْهو حولَكَ،

تدْعو الأشياءَ إلى اللهوِ...
بهذا، تعرفُها أكثَرَ،
تصبحُ أفكارَكَ أكثرَ من قبْلُ،
تَنَزَّهْ بين الأفكارِ،

ودَعْها تتنزَّهُ مثلَكَ،
واجْعَلْ نَسَباً،
يقْوى،
يتنامى،
بين الأفكارِ وبين الأشياءْ.

— 3 —

لا شيْءَ يقودُكَ كالكلماتْ.
هي أفكارٌ كالأشياءِ،
وأشياءٌ كالأفكارِ،
هي الأشكالُ، الألوانُ،
هي النُّزْهةُ ...
لا شيْءَ يقودُكَ، حُرّاً، كالكلماتْ.

— 7 —

يجري الوقتُ،
فلا يحتاجُ إلى مجرىً.
ولو احتاجَ لكانَ لِمَجْراهُ ضِفافٌ،
يرْتَعُ فيها النسيانْ.
لو كان الأمرُ كذلكَ،
ما قُلْنا: لو كانَ،
ولو كانَ،
ولو كانْ.

— 8 —

ليس الحاضرُ إلا حَجَراً،
يرْكلُهُ الماضي،
يجعلُهُ،

كالعثْرةِ،
في أقدام المستقبلْ.

— 9 —

تاريخٌ يُروى،
كي نتذكَّرَ،
ليت لنا تاريخاً
يُروى،
كي ننْسى ...

— 11 —

يُزْعِجُكَ التدخينُ،
وقد دخَنْتَ كثيراً.
دخَنْتَ وما زِلْتَ تُدَخِّنُ،
تحْسَبُ أنَّكَ تعترِضُ الوقتَ،
فتجْعلُهُ يُبْطِئُ،
تحْسَبُ أنَّكَ تعْتقِلُ اللحْظةَ بالتدخينِ،
تُسائلُها،
تَنْفُثُ فيها بعضَ رسائلَ،
ثم تُحرِّرُها،
تُطْلِقُها في جَوٍّ يُصبحُ مشْحوناً بِكَ،
لكنَّكَ تُقْلِعُ أحياناً،

تُقْلِعُ دوْماً،
تُقْلِعُ ثم تعودُ،
تُدَخِّنُ كي لا يغْدرَكَ الوقتُ فيمْضي دونَكَ ...
يُزْعِجُكَ التدخينُ،

ولكنْ، من يحضنُ أوهامَكَ؟
يَسْتعْبِدُكَ التدخين،
وتحْسَبُ أنّكَ تَسْتعْبِدُهُ.
تعتادُ عليهِ فتعتادُ على نفْسِكَ،
تُقْلِعُ عنهُ فتُقْلِعُ عنكَ،
وحين تعودُ إليهِ تعودُ إليكَ ...
هي اللحْظةُ توثِّقُها، كي تعترِضَ الوقتَ،
دخانُكَ بعضُ رسائلَ

منكَ إلى غيبٍ ليس يُهادِنُ ...
يُزْعِجُكَ التدخينُ،
ولكنّكَ دخّنْتَ وما زِلْتَ:
تُدَخِّنُ، تُقْلِعُ، ثم تُدَخِّنُ ...
أيّامُكَ تُشْبِهُ أيّامَكَ،
والعالَمُ حوْلَكَ أوهامٌ
ودخانْ.

_ 20 _

حجَرٌ،
يسْقطُ في الماءِ،
يغوصُ إلى القَعْرِ،
ولكنّ دوائرَ تظْهَرُ في وجْهِ الماءِ،
دوائرَ خَلْفَ دوائرَ تنشأ من نفْسِ النقطةِ،
تبدأ ضَيِّقةً،
تتسارعُ أوْسَعَ أوْسَعَ نحو الأطرافِ،
تُدغدغُ وجْهَ الماءِ،
فتجْعلهُ يتجهَّمُ،
أو يتبسَّمْ.

_ 22 _

يتقاطعُ خطّانِ،
فإذْ بهما ينطلقانِ،
كما لم ينطلقا من قبْلُ،
لأنهما قد وقعا في النقْطةِ ...
يتّجهانِ كما كانا من قبْلُ،
ولكنْ مُرْتبِكيْنِ،
فتنأى جهةُ الأوّلِ عن جهةِ الآخَرِ،
تتّسعُ الهُوّةُ بيْنهما،
لكنّ الواحدَ يبقى مشدوداً لغواياتِ الآخَرِ،
في أحوالِ النقْطةْ.

_ 24 _

ينْبسِطُ الوقتُ كسَهْلٍ جارٍ.
يُبْطِئُ أحياناً،
يُسْرِعُ أحياناً،
أمَا الشِعْرُ فيُنْبِتُ فيهِ بعضَ الأشجارِ،
ليُوقِفَهُ أحياناً ...

(ربيع 2021)

Jawdat Fakhreddine is a Lebanese poet and professor emeritus of Arabic literature at the Lebanese University in Beirut. He was born in 1953 in a small village in southern Lebanon. He is currently based in Beirut. He has published over ten poetry collections and two works of literary criticism. He regularly contributed to newspapers and journals across the Arab world. His collection of children's poems, *Thirty Poems for Children*, won the Sheikh Zayed Book Award for that category in 2014. His poetry has been translated to French, German, and English. Translated works include *Lighthouse of the Drowning* (BOA Editions, 2017) and *The Sky that Denied Me* (University of Texas Press, 2020).

Selections from "Intersections" by Jawdat Fakhreddine

Translated by Huda Fakhreddine

1.
The expanding field invites you
to an expanding view,
but a tree rises up
and invites you to look into yourself,
where the real secrets are,
without saints or conjurers.

2.
Let your thoughts sit next to you like things,
even if they were confused or cloudy.
Things are like that too,
no matter how clear and settled they may seem.
Befriend your thoughts and trust them,
even if they wander, change, and scatter.
Things are like that too,
no matter how still they may seem.
Release your thoughts from your head.

Let them frolic around you.
Let them invite things to play.
Your thoughts will be more
than before
when you stroll among them
and let them stroll too.
Let there be a bond,
a kinship that extends
and grows
between thought and thing.

3.
Nothing guides you like words.

Words are thoughts like things,
and things like thoughts.
They are shape and color,
a promenade.
Nothing leads you free like words.

7.
Time flows
without a course.
If it needed one, it would also
need banks
where forgetfulness lolled.
If it were like that,
we would never have said: if only,
if only,
if only.

8.
The present is but a stone
that the past kicks,
a stumbling block
for the future
to trip on.

9.
History is told
for us to remember.
If only we had a history
Told for us
 to forget.

11.
Smoking bothers you
and you've smoked a lot.
You smoke and smoke,

thinking you can interject time,
slow it down.
You think you can arrest the moment
in smoke, question it,
breathe into it messages,
then let it go,
releasing it into the air,
now charged with you.
But you quit sometimes.
You always quit,
quit and return.
You smoke so time won't deceive you
and go on without you….
Smoking bothers you
but who else will embrace your illusions?
Smoking enslaves you
and you think you enslave it.
You get used to it to get used to yourself.
You quit it to quit yourself.
And when you return to it,
you return to yourself.
It is a moment you preserve to interject time.
Your smoke is but the signals you send
to a relentless unknown.
Smoking bothers you,
but you smoke and smoke.
You smoke and quit, and smoke again.
Your days are your days, all the same,
and the world around you
illusion and smoke.

20.
Into the water,
a stone
drops
and sinks,

but the circles that appear
on the water's face
radiating out, circle after circle
and then retreat.
They hurry toward the edges
stroking water's face
into a frown
or smile.

22.
Two lines intersect
and suddenly they launch
like never before.
And that's because
they have fallen to the point…
They proceed as they were
but confused,
each heading in a different direction.
The gap between them grows,
but one remains drawn to the other's temptations
and to the dispositions of the point.

24.
Time extends like a rolling field.
It slows sometimes
and hurries sometimes.
But poetry sprouts in it trees
and stops it sometimes.

Huda Fakhreddine is the author of *Metapoesis in the Arabic Tradition* (Brill, 2015) and *The Arabic Prose Poem: Poetic Theory and Practice* (Edinburgh University Press, 2021). Her translations of Arabic poems have appeared in *Banipal, World Literature Today, Nimrod, ArabLit Quarterly, Middle Eastern Literatures*, among others. She is associate professor of Arabic literature at the University of Pennsylvania.

نشيد الحياة

آدم فتحي

لَنْ يَمُوتَ لِأَجْلِهَا مِنَّا أَحَدْ
كي لا نموت لوحدنا

لاَ

لَنْ يَمُوتَ لِأَجْلِهَا مِنَّا أَحَدْ
كَيْ لاَ يَعِيشُوا وحْدَهُمْ مِنْ بَعْدِنَا

لاَ

لن يموت صباحها الأحلى
وإن طال السوادُ

هذي البِلادُ لنَا وإنْ كَرِهُوا وكادُوا
ولنا طفولةُ حُلْمِها ولنا الحصادُ

ولنا ضجيجُ زِحامِها الخالي
حروفُ الطَّقسِ في دمِها
دبيبُ النَّاس
داخِلَ صَمْتِها وعُرُوقِها
الشَّهْدُ المُكَوَّرُ
في صُدُورِ بَناتِها
أسنانُها اللَّبَنِيَّةُ الأولَى
أَزِقَّتُها التي يَبْرِي السُّهادُ

هذي البلاد لنا وإن كرهوا وكادوا
ولنا طفولة حلمها ولنا الحصاد

ولنا تَبَتُّلُنا على أسوارِها الأَعْلَى
وأنَّا قد فَرَشْنا قَبْلَ جِلْدِ الثَّورِ
جِلْدَتَنا
على حَصْباءِ سُمْرَتِها
وقَبَّلْنا
فضاءَ الجَمْرِ في يَدِها
وعَلَّمْنَا
خُطَى الأهرامِ أن تَخْضَرَّ في غَدِها
وأنْ تَرْقَى بِمَجْرَدَةٍ
إلى أكتافِ دِجْلَتِها
ولَمْ نَصْنَعْ خِيامَ صِغارِها
مِنْ شَعرِ جازِيَةِ الهِلالِيِّينَ
بل مِمَّا يُكابِدُهُ الفُؤادُ

هذي البلادُ لنا وإنْ كرِهوا وكادوا
ولنا طفولةُ حلمها ولنا الحصادُ

فلْيُمْطِروا حَصْباءَها جَمْرًا
إذا عَزَّ المَطَرْ

ولْيُوقِدُوا في عُشْبِ ليلتِها أصابِعَنا
إذا ذَبُلَ القَمَرْ

ولْيَزْرَعُوا حاناتِها بالأنبياءْ
وقِبابَها بِالخَيْلِ والعَسْكَرْ

لَهُمْ أن يُثْخِنُوها كَيْفَما شاؤُوا
فنحنُ لها الضِّمادُ

هذي البِلادُ لنا وإنْ كَرِهُوا وكادُوا
ولنا طفولةُ حُلْمِها ولنا الحَصادُ

لا شَيْءَ فيها مِثْلَما نَهْوَى ولا نَهْوَى سِواها
هكذا:
بِشُقُوقِ خُضْرَتِها وحُلْكَةِ صَمْتِها وسُدَى خُطاها

بِطَنِينِ نَحْلَتِها الفَصِيحْ
بِأَكُفَّ فَلَّاحاتِها في الرِّيحْ

بِصُوفَةِ يَوْمِها البالِي
وسِدْرَةِ مُنْتَهاها

لا شَيْءَ فيها مِثْلَما نَهْوَى ولا نَهْوَى سِواها

هكذا:

بِنَخِيلِها النَّاعِسْ
بِسَقْفِ جِراحِها العالِي
إذَا ضاقَ المُباحْ
بِنَمْلِها اليَوْمِيِّ يَحْفِرُ خُبْزَهُ

بِجبالِها وجُيوبِها
بِشمالِها وجنوبِها

بِالرِّيفِ صبرِ الريفِ في الدمِ والخَريفِ

بِقاعِها
وشِراعِها

بِشوارعِ الحُرِّيَّةِ المُلقاةِ دومًا في خرائطِها
إلي نَفْسِ الأزِقَّةِ

بِالتَّماثِيلِ المُقيمةِ
والتي تَمْشي
على

أحلامِنا

وبِوَرْدةٍ تَخْفَى
فيَفْضَحُها
شَذاها

لا شَيْءَ فيها مِثْلَما نَهْوَى ولا نَهْوَى سِواها

هكذا:

بعمَى حمُورابي الجديد عن الغد المحفوظ في الألواح

هكذا:

بِخُروج آدمَ من جنائنها
ولم تلمس يداهُ حلاوةَ التُّفَّاح

بِقصائدِ الشَّابِّي التي خجلت
بلهفة من يسمّيها
ويحسب أنَّنا أشباح
بِجَفافِ ماءِ القلب

بِضَياع هانيبالْ
يَزُفُّ الأطْلَسِي للألبْ

وبِطَيْرِ بابِ البَحْرِ وهو يُعيدُ خَلْقَ البَحْر
كُلَّ عَشِيَّةٍ

يا طَيْرَ بابِ البَحْرِ قُلْ لِي

أين صاحِبُكَ القديمُ
وأين راحَ جوادُهُ المُتَنَطِّعُ

يا طَيرَ بابِ البَحْرِ قُلْ لِي

بَدَّلوهُ بِساعةٍ
سَتَعِيشُ ساعتَها وتَمْضِي
أمْ هوَ السَّرْجُ القديمُ مُجَدَّدًا لا يُخْلَعُ

يا طَيرَ بابِ البَحْرِ قُلْ هذي البِلادَ كما نَراها

قُلْ شَوْقَها للماء
قُلْ غدَها الذي لم يَتْرُكُونا
نشْتَهِيه كما نَشاء
قُلْ ظلَّ هذا الذُّلِّ
قُلْ يَدَها على أكْبادِها
قُلْ صَمتَها
قُلْ مِحْنَةَ الشُّعَراء إنْ هُمْ عانَقُوا شَكْواها
قُلْ كُلَّ أغْلِفةِ القذائفِ في جُيُوبِ رُماتِها
وهُمْ على أبوابِ غَفْلَتِها
لِغَصْبِ رِضاهَا

قُلْ كَمْ غدًا وَشَّتْ
لِيَخْتَلِسُوا رُبَاهُ

وكَمْ فَتًى عَشَّتْ
لِيَفْتَرِسُوا خُطَاهُ

وكَمْ بَلاهَا البَحْرُ والبَحّارُ
كَمْ جابَتْ
وكَمْ خابَتْ
وكَمْ خاطَتْ ضُلوعَ جِراحِها
لِتَظلَّ أقْوَى

لَم يُعَلِّم فُلْكَها حِزْبٌ طَريقَ البَرِّ
لَم يَحدبْ عليها صاحِبٌ
لَمْ يَحمِها خَشَبٌ
عَداهَا

يا طَيْرَ بابِ البَحْرِ قُلْ هذي البِلادَ كما نَراها

قُلْ حُلمَها المَكْسُور
سوف نَقُولُه
ونَقُولُها
ونَقُولُ للمُتَكَحِّلِينَ بِطُولِ ما انْتَظرَتْ رَحِيلَ دُجاهَا
سنَظلُّ نَهواها بِكُمْ
أنْتُمْ
فَساد الحُبِّ
أخشابًا بِلا وَتَدِ
وأعدادًا بِلا عَدَدِ
وأصحابًا بِلا مَدَدِ
وأحزابًا
بَدَتْ في غَيْرِ مَوْضِعِها دُمًى
تَحْكِي انتِفاخًا صَوْلَةَ الأَسَدِ

ويَغْلبُها الرُّقادُ
كَمْ ثَبَتْنَا حيثُ فَرُّوا
كَمْ ألفَنَا قول يحيَا كُلَّمَا ظَهَرُوا ومَرُّوا
ثمَّ مِتْنَا ثمّ عِشْنَا ثمّ مِتْنَا كي يُسَرُّوا

صَدِّقُوا الشُّعَراءْ
أمَا قُلْنَا لَكُمْ هُوَ ذا الجَرادُ

هذي البِلادُ لَنا وإنْ كَرِهُوا وكادُوا

ولَنا طُفولةٌ حُلْمِها ولَنا الحَصادُ
فلْيُقْنِعُونا بِانتحارِ اللّيْلِ شَنْقًا
في صفيحِ نِعالِهم
وبِأنَّ أشجارَ القُرَى
تَمْشي على أغصانِهِمْ
وبِأنَّ مِنْ طَبْعِ الخُطَى هذا التَّقَدُّمَ لِلوَراءْ
وبِأنَّ أكواخَ البِلادِ
بَلابِلٌ حَطَّتْ لِيَفْقِسَ بَيْضُهُمْ
وبِأنَّ ماءَ البَحرِ أحْلَى مِنْ دَمِ الحَلْوَى
على شَفَةِ الوَلِيدْ

قُدَّامَ كَأسِ النّارِ سَوْفَ نَلُمُّ وَرْدَ نِسائِنا
ونَقُولُ لا
لا ليس هذا مَا نُريدْ

تَخْبُو ذُؤاباتُ الدُّموعْ
تَذْوي الشَّوارعُ والشُّموعْ
تَغْشَى العشايَا والعَواصِمُ والعُيون
ونحنُ نحنْ

هَلْ هذه أحْلامُنا

ألِهذه الجُزُرِ الكَئِيبَةِ
أبْحَرَتْ آلامُنا

وعَلامَ كانَ لِكُلِّ هذا أنْ يَكُونْ

مِنْ خَيْبَةٍ نَمْضِي إلى أخرَى
ونَمْضِي
كي نَعُودْ

هل كانت الصّحراءُ كي تَعْيَى بِنا الأمطارُ في هذي السّحابةُ
هل كانَ مَا قُلْنَا لِيَفْهَمَنَا فَقَطْ جَيْشُ الرَّقابةْ

لا ليس هذا ما نُريدْ

أَبَدًا يَظلُّ أمامَنا أُفقٌ نُوَبِّنُهُ ومَوَّالٌ شَريدْ

ونُحِبُّ أَنْ نَحْيَا الحياةْ
ونُحِبُّ أَنْ نَرِثَ الجِهاتِ
ونُحِبُّ أن نعِيَ الجَليدْ

ونُحِبُّ أيضًا أَنْ نُحِبَّ
وأن نُحَبَّ
وأَنْ يَكُونَ لِقَشِّنَا عُشٌّ سَعيدْ

أين الفَرَحْ
أين النَّشيدْ

هل هذه أحلامُنا
لا ليس هذا ما نُريدْ

وَطَني أمامَ كَمينِهِ قال البَلَحْ

وَطَني بَعيدْ
وَطَني جَميلْ
وَطَني جَميلٌ في العُيُونْ
وَطَني جَميلٌ في عُيُونِ الآخَرينْ

ولأنَّهُ وَطَني أنَا
ولأنَّ جَنْبًا عاشَ يَفْتَرِشُ الحَصَى والشَّوْكَ في طُرُقاتِهِ

جَنْبِي أَنَا
سَأَظَلُّ أَحْلُمُ أَنَّهُ وَطَنٌ
وَأَنْظُرُ لِلْبَعِيدْ

هل هذه أحلامُنا

أَنْ يَرْتَدِي ذِئْبُ البَرارِي
لِحْيَةً رَقْطَاءْ
وَأَنْ يَرْقَى الفَحِيحُ إلى نَشِيدْ

هل هذه أحلامُنا

أَنْ تُطْبَخَ الأحلامُ في نُسَخٍ وتُعرَض
في طُبُولٍ مِنْ حَدِيدْ

فكَأَنَّ هذا الخَسَّ مُلْتَفًّا على أوراقِهِ
صُحُفٌ
كَأَنَّ تَوَجُّعَ الأنهارِ إيذانٌ بِفَتْحِ الرَّقْصِ
فَوقَ قُبُورِ مَوْتَانَا
كَأَنَّ البرلمانْ
بَرُّ الأمانْ
كَأَنَّهُ وَطَنٌ
كَأَنَّا لَمْ يَعُدْ فِينَا عَبِيدْ

لا ليس هذا ما نُرِيد

ونُرِيدُ مَا شَهِدَ الشَّهِيدُ
بِأَنَّهُ القَدَرُ المُرادْ

هذي البِلادُ لَنا وإنْ كَرِهُوا وكادُوا
ولَنا طُفولةُ حُلْمِها ولَنا الحَصادْ

ماذا تَغَيَّرَ في الحياةِ
وفي الفُصُولِ وفي الجِهاتِ
وفي الجِبالِ وفي الهُوِيّ

ماذا تَغَيَّرَ في الطَّوابِي والقُرَى
ماذا تَغَيَّرَ في جُحُورِ الزَّنْكِ
والأَلْيافِ
والسَّعَفِ الطَّرِيّ

ماذا تَغَيَّرَ في عَشايَا السَّبْتِ
حِينَ تَضُمُّ بِنْتُ الفَقْرِ وِحْشَتَها
ويَرْتَجِفُ الصَّبِيّ

ماذا تَغَيَّرَ في صَباحاتِ الأحدْ
ماذا تَغَيَّرَ في ضُحَى الإثْنينِ أو لَيْلِ الخميسْ

لا ظِلَّ فَوْقَ تَحَجُّرِ الأحجارِ غَيْرَ ظِلالِهِمْ
لا كَفَّ حَوْلَ تَكَوُّرِ الأثمارِ غَيْرَ أكُفِّهمْ
لا وَجْهَ في حِبْرِ الجرائدِ
في الهواءِ الرَّثِّ
في زيتِ الخُطى
أو خلفَ بلّورِ التّليفزيونِ
غَيْرَ وُجُوهِهِمْ
أو مَا تَحَوَّلَ مِنْ مَلامِحِنا
إلى قَمَرٍ خَصِيّ

حتّى لَنَسْألُ أينَ نَحنْ
لَكَأَنَّنا شَعبٌ خَفِيّ

ماذا تَغَيَّرَ
كَيْ نُعِيِّدَ

أو نُؤَيِّدَ
أو نَرَى قِطَعًا مِنَ البِسْكُوتِ
في هذي العِصِيُّ

كُنَّا نُصَدِّقُ عِيدَهُمْ لَوْ كانَ عِيدَا
كُنَّا نُقَبِّلُ نَجْمَهُمْ
لَوْ لَمْ يَكُنْ دَمُنَا على فَمِنَا شَهِيدَا

فَلْيَبْحَثُوا عن غَيْمَةٍ أُخرَى
وعن كَمَّاشة أخرى
وعَنَّا آخَرِينْ
كي ينطلِي مَا لَمْ يُؤَمِّنْ كَأسَهُ
حتَّى الجَمادُ

هذي البِلادُ لَنا وإنْ كَرِهُوا وكادُوا
ولَنا طُفولةُ حُلْمِها ولَنا الحَصادُ

وسنَعْبُرُ الصَّحراءْ

سيَخْتَرِعُونَ ضِدَّ جُنُونِنا بالأرض
عَقْلاً عاقِلاً جِدًّا
وحَقًّا مائِلاً جِدًّا
وقَصْرًا في السَّماءْ

ولأنَّنا لا نَشْتَهِي مَا يُشْتَهى
سيَتَرْجِمُونَ صُراخَنا ثَلْبًا
لِزَقزَقَةِ النَّسِيمِ على خُيوطِ الكَهرباءْ
وسيَهْمِسُونَ بِأَنَّنا أَصْلاً
نُحِبُّ جَمالَنا أسْرَى وخَلْفَ الظِّلِّ نَهوانَا

سيَخْتَرِفُونَ تَعْبِيدَ المَسالِكِ في مَسامِّ جُلودِنا جِدًّا

ويَحْتَرِفُونَ مِنْ بَعْدُ الرِّثاءْ

وسنَعْبُرُ الصّحراءْ

سيَصْطادُونَنا في كُلِّ زاوِيَةٍ
وَراءَ الباب
في حَلَقاتِنا الخضراءْ

سنَحْمِلُ حُبَّنَا في صُرَّةٍ
ودِماءُ قَتْلانَا عَصانَا

نَعْبُرُ الصّحراءْ

لأنّا لا نَرَى وَسْطَ الخَراب
خَيْمَةٌ
ولا نَحْنُو على هذا السَّراب
لِنَبُوسَ بَيْنَ يَدَيْه
خَدَّ صَبِيَّةٍ
أو رَأْسَ حَلْمَةٌ

نَعْبُرُ الصّحراءَ دُونَ جِيادِنا
إمّا بَراهَا اللَّيْلُ أو سَقَطَتْ بِنَا

ونُعارِضُ الرَّمْلَ المُسافِرَ في العُيُون
نُعارِضُ الغَضَبَ المُتَوَّجَ بالسُّكُون
نُعارِضُ الدَّمَ إنْ غدا كالماء صلْبَا

وعلى حريقِ العشب
سوف يخطِّ ومضُ جراحنا

إنْ لَمْ يُعِدَّ الشَّعْبُ مِنْ أشلائِنا دَرْبَا
أو كان أصْغَرَ مِنْ حرائقِ عُمْرِنا

سنُعارِضُ الشَّعبَا
ونَنْهَضُ حيثُما سقطت جيادُ

هذي البِلادُ لَنا وإنْ كَرِهُوا وكادُوا
ولَنا طُفولةُ حُلْمِها ولَنا الحَصادُ

ولَهُمْ هُنَا أَنْ يَخْتِمُوا أَفْواهَنا بِالشَّمْعِ
إنْ صَرَخَتْ حَذارِ

وأَنْ يَدُقُّوها أَصابِعَنا إذا كسرت خَوابِيَهُمْ
بِمِسْمارِ

وأَنْ يَقِفُوا يتامَي
إِنْ تَهَدَّلَ سَقْفُهُمْ
أو خَرَّ تمثالٌ
وبَدَّلَ قِشْرَهُ جَلَّادُ

سنَعِيشُ في رِيشِ الجَناحِ
إذا أَطاحَ بِنَا العَرِيشْ
ونُحِبُّ كُلَّ دَقيقةٍ
أَلاَّ نَمُوتَ لِكي نَعِيشْ

نُحِبُّ أَنْ يَسْمَرَّ نَجْمُ الرِّيفِ في يَدِنَا
بِعِطْرِ المَوْجِ
أَنْ تُقْشَى صناديقُ اللُّصوصِ
لِكَيْ يَعُودَ دمُ البِلادِ لأَهْلِهَا
ويَسِيلَ وَرْدُ الحَقْلِ مِن خَزَفِ القُصورِ
إلي مواويلِ الرُّعاةْ

سنُحِبُّ أَنْ تَصِلَ العصافيرُ الطَّرِيدَة
مِنْ نوافِذِها البَعِيدة

أن تُغَنِّيَ دُونَ أَنْ تُرْمَى
بِقُفْلٍ
أو حَصاةٌ

أن تستطيع البنتُ في ضوضاء باب البحر
أن تَخْتَارَ بَحْرَ حَبِيبِهَا
وتَمسّ رُكْبَتَهُ الرقيقة
دُونَ أن تخشى الوُشاةُ

أن يكسُوَ العُمَّالُ صِبْيَتَهُمْ ويَمْضُوا
لاقتِناء روائع الرَّسْمِ المُعاصِرِ

أنْ تُسافِرَ صابةُ الفَلَّاحِ مِنْ نعناع كأسِ الشَّايْ
إلى دُورِ الثَّقافة

أَنْ يَرى الشُّعراءُ في وَرَقِ التُّرابِ
سُطُورَهُمْ تَخْضَرُّ

أنْ يَمْتَدَّ نَخْلُ عُروقِنَا
مِنْ ماءِ دجْلةَ والفُرات
إلى سواحِلَ
لا يُحاصِرها قَراصِنَةُ الحياةِ

ونُحِبُّهُمْ
عَارِينَ أَكْثَرَ

هذه أحلامُنا

لا
لن يَلِينَ لها قِيادُ
هذي البِلادُ لَنَا وإنْ كَرِهُوا وكادُوا

ولَنا طُفولةُ حُلْمِها ولَنا الحَصادُ

لا

لَنْ يَمُوتَ لِأَجْلِهَا مِنَّا أَحَدْ
كي لا نموت
لِوَحْدِنا

لاَ

لن يموت لأجلها منّا أحد
كي لا يعيشوا وحدهم
من بَعْدِنا

لا

لن يموت لأجلها منّا أحدْ
فالميِّتُونَ لِأَجْلِهَا
أَحْياؤُنَا

لا

لَمْ يَعُدْ لِلمَوْتِ وَقْت

سنَعِيشُ وقْتَنا ثانِيًا
في كُلِّ مَوتْ

نصف الغيوم
ونَقْلَعُ الأشواكَ
من هذا الجسَدْ

سنَعِيشُ يَوْما ثانِيًا كَيْدًا لَهُمْ
في كُلِّ يَوْمْ
حتَّي الأَبَدْ

فلْيُطْفِئُونَا في حَرائِقِ حُلْمِنا
ولْيُحْرِقُونَا في حَدائِقِ عُمْرِنا

سيَظَلُّ يَبْعَثُنا الرَّمادُ

هذي البِلادُ لَنا وإنْ كَرِهُوا وكادُوا
ولَنا طُفولةُ حُلْمِها ولَنا الحَصادُ

Fathi Gasmi, better known by his pen name **Adam Fethi**, is one of the most celebrated poets of dissent in Tunisia. He was born October 3rd, 1957 in the south of the country. His poetry of commitment, written under the siege of the political repression in the 1970s and 1990s, fought for freedom of thought and expression. He channeled his protest into several songs, which enhanced his popularity among students. He is the author of *Ughniat al-Naqabi al-Fasih* (*Song of the Eloquent Unionist,* 1986), *Anachid li Zahrat al-Ghubar* (*Songs For the Dust Rose,* 1991) and *Nafikhu al-Zujaj al-A'maa* (*The Blind Glassblower,* 2011), which won the prestigious Abou Kacem Chebbi Prize (2012). Adam Fethi received the Sargon Boulus award for poetry and translation in 2019.

The Song of Life

Translated by Hager Ben Driss

None of us will die for her;
Otherwise, we will be the only ones to die.

No.

None of us will die for her;
Otherwise, they will be the only ones to survive.

No.

Her sweetest morning will not die
despite the protracted darkness.

This country is ours even if they deny it and connive.
We own her early dreams, and for the harvest we shall strive.

We own the noise of the empty crowd,
the letters of the climate in her blood,
the crawl of people
inside her silence and veins,
the rounded honey
in her daughters' breasts,
her first milk tooth,
her insomniac feeble alleys.

This country is ours even if they deny it and connive.
We own her early dreams, and for the harvest we shall strive.

Our devotion: on her highest walls.
Prior to the bull skin[1],

---

[1]. Reference to the legend of the founding of Carthage.

we spread out our skin
on the gravel of her tan,
kissed
the embers in her hand,
taught
the pyramid steps to become verdant in her tomorrow
and to lift Medjerda to
Dejla's shoulder;
we didn't make her children's tents
out of al-Jazia al-Hilalia's hair,
but with the endurance of our hearts.

This country is ours even if they deny it and connive.
We own her early dreams, and for the harvest we shall strive.

Let them shower her pebbles with embers
if rain is scarce.

Let them ignite our fingers to burn the grass of her night
if the moon withers.

Let them sow prophets in her taverns;
horses and soldiers in her domes.

Let them wound her however they please;
we will be her bandage.

This country is ours even if they deny it and connive.
We own her early dreams, and for the harvest we shall strive.

Nothing about her is seductive, but she is the one we desire.

That's it.

We love the fissures of her verdure, the darkness of her silence, the futility of her steps,
the eloquent buzz of her bee,

the female farmers' palms in the wind,

the wool of her shabby day,
and her Lote-Tree of the Furthest Boundary.

Nothing about her is seductive, but she is the one we desire.

That's it.

We love her dozing palm trees,
the high ceiling of her wounds
when the permissible shrinks,
her common ants foraging for food,

her mountains and entrances,
her north and south,

autumn and the patience of the countryside in the blood,

her bottom
and sail,

the Liberté avenues always scattered on her maps,
naming the same alleys,
the frozen statues
only treading
on our dreams,

a hiding flower
betrayed by her fragrance.

Nothing about her is seductive, but she is the one we desire.

That's it.

We love her with the new Hammurabi's blindness to the future preserved

in a tablet,
Adam's expulsion from her gardens
before he could reach the sweetness of apples,

Al-Shabbi's embarrassed poems,
the zeal of those who name her
and think of us as ghosts,

the desiccate heart,

Hannibal's demise
as he wedded the Atlantic to the Alps,

and the birds of Bab Bhar[2] recreating the sea
every evening.

O birds of Bab Bhar tell me,

where's your old friend
and where's his pretentious horse gone?[3]

O birds of Bab Bhar tell me,
did they exchange it with a clock,
that will live for a while and leave,
or is it the same old saddle anew, impossible to renew?

O Birds of Bab Bhar speak about this country the way we see it.
Speak about her longing for water.
Speak about her tomorrow, forbidden
to be desired in the way we desire.

---

2. Bab Bhar, literally the Sea Gate, is the gate to the old *medina* of Tunis.
3. Reference to the statue of former President, Habib Bourguiba, which was exchanged with a clock after the November 7th, 1987 and the ascension of Zine al-Abadine Ben Ali to power.

Speak about the shadow of this disgrace.
Speak about her protective hand on her children.
Speak about her silence.
Speak about the poets' ordeal when they embrace her grievance.
Speak about the shells in the pockets of her shooters,
standing by the doors of her inadvertence
to force her hand.

Speak about the many tomorrows she embellished
to be stolen,

and the many lads she nourished
to be devoured.

Speak about how sea and sailor harmed her,

how long she wandered,
how disappointed she was,
how she stitched the sides of her wound
to stay strong.

No party showed her ship the land,
no friend gave her a hand,
no wood protected her.

O Birds of Bab Bhar speak about this country the way we see it.

Say, we're going to speak about
her broken dream
and her.
We'll tell those who are delighted to see her waiting for a bright day:
we'll keep loving her despite
you,
the corrupt love,
timbers without a pole,
numberless numbers,

uncharitable friends,
and misplaced parties
like puppets
who boast about the lion's power
and then fall asleep.

We stood fast where they deserted,
we got used to "long live …!" whenever they appeared.
We died and lived, then died again to make them happy.

Trust the poets.
Didn't we tell you these are locusts?

This country is ours even if they deny it and connive.
We own her early dreams, and for the harvest we shall strive.

Let them convince us that the night
strangled itself with the laces of their shoes,
that the trees of villages
walk on their branches,
that steps are disposed to progress backwards,
that the shacks of the country
are bulbuls waiting for their eggs to hatch,
that the sea water is sweeter than the blood of candies
on the newborn's lip.

Face to the cup of fire, we will gather our women's flowers
and say, No.
No, this is not what we want.

Comets of tears fade out,
streets and candles shiver,
evenings, cities, and eyes go blind.

And what about us?

Are these our dreams?

Did our sorrow sail to these desolate islands?

And why did all of this happen?

We move from one disappointment to the next.
We only proceed to recede.

Was it the desert in that cloud
that made the rain so tired?
Did we speak solely to be understood by an army of censors?

No, this is not what we want.

There will always be a horizon to lament
and a homeless roundelay ahead.

We love to live life.
We love to inherit directions.
We love to comprehend ice.

And we also love to love,
to be loved,
and make a happy nest for our straw.
Where is joy?
Where is the song?

Are these our dreams?
No, this is not what we want.

The dates say: My homeland is snared;

my homeland is far away;
my homeland is beautiful;
my homeland's beauty catches the eye;
my homeland's beauty is in the eye of the beholder.

And because it's *my* homeland,

because a body has spent a lifetime laying on its roads' pebbles and thorns,
and that body happens to be mine,
I will dream of it as my homeland
and look far away.

Are these our dreams?

To see the prairie wolf
grow a dappled beard,
or to elevate hissing to the status of singing?

Are these our dreams?

To replicate cooked dreams and display them
in iron drums?

As if the folded lettuce
were newspaper leaves,
as if the rivers' suffering heralds the season of dancing
on the graves of the dead,
as if the parliament
were a safe haven,
as if it were a homeland,
as if we had ceased to be slaves.

No, this is not what we want.

We want what the martyr confirmed
 as the desired fate.

This country is ours even if they deny it and connive.
We own her early dreams, and for the harvest we shall strive.

What has changed in life,
in seasons and directions,
in mountains and abysses?

What has changed in fortresses and villages?
What has changed in the zinc,
fiber,
and soft frond dens?

What has changed on Saturday evenings
when a destitute girl embraces her desolation
and a young boy shivers?

What has changed on Sunday mornings?
What has changed on Monday afternoons or Thursday evenings?

No shadow on the rocky stones but theirs;
no palm around ripe fruits but theirs;
no faces in newspapers,
the shabby air,
the greasy steps,
or TV screen
but theirs
or our features
morphed into a castrated moon.

So much so that we wonder where we are,
as if we were invisible.

What has changed for us
so that we celebrate,
approve
or see carrots
in these sticks?

We'd believe in their celebrations
if they were real.
We'd kiss their star
if our blood was not still warm in our mouths.
Let them look for another cloud,
other pliers,

and other 'us'
who'd fall for a cup[4]
that even objects don't trust.

This country is ours even if they deny it and connive.
We own her early dreams, and for the harvest we shall strive.
And, yes, we will cross the desert.

To counteract our crazy love for the land,
they will invent a very reasonable reason,
a very twisted truth,
and a castle in the sky.

Because we want something different,
they will translate our rant into a slander
of the faint breeze on electric wires;
they will whisper that we actually
like to see our beauty captive,
and long to see ourselves overcast.

They will excel at paving tracks in our pores
and then excel at lamentation.

We will cross the desert.

They will pursue us around every corner,
behind the door,
and in our green circles.

We'll wrap our love in a bundle; the blood of the dead our stick.
We cross the desert

because we can't see a tent among these ruins,
we can't bend on this mirage
to kiss a girl's cheek

---

4. Allusion to the cup of poison Socrates was obliged to drink.

or a nipple's tip.

We cross the desert without our horses
which have either been bridled by the night
or have fallen over.

We oppose the sand travelling in the eyes.
We oppose anger crowned with silence.
We oppose blood if it solidifies like water.

We will inscribe the blaze of our wounds
on the burning grass.

If the people fail to pave a road out of our dismembered limbs,
or if they prove smaller than the fires of our lives,
we will oppose them,
and rise just where our horses fell.
This country is ours even if they deny it and connive.
We own her early dreams, and for the harvest we shall strive.

They can shut our mouths
if they shout "Beware!",

hammer our fingers,
if they break their jars, like a nail;

stand up like orphans
if their roof dangles,
or a statue collapses
and a tyrant erects another in its stead.

We will live in the feathers of the wing
if the tree rejects us,
and every second will
brave death to exist.

We want to hold the star of the countryside

and watch it tan in the scent of the sea;
we want the thieves' boxes disclosed
so that the blood of the land returns to the people of the land,
and the flowers of the fields flow out of the castles' ceramics
back to the shepherds.

We want the evicted birds from their distant windows
to reach their destination,

and sing
without being stoned
or encaged.

We want girls to pick their sweethearts
Amid the din of Bab Bhar,
and touch their soft knees
without fear of slander.

We want the workers to clothe their children and then
buy contemporary paintings, masterpieces.

We want the farmer's crop to travel from kitchens
to arts centers.

We want poets to see their lines
turn green on the soil's paper.

We want the palm trees of our veins to stretch
from Baghdad's lovely water
to coasts free of life's pirates.

And, yes, we want them to be more naked.

These are our dreams.

No,
they will never comply.

This country is ours even if they deny it and connive.
We own her early dreams, and for the harvest we shall strive.

None of us will die for her;
Otherwise, we will be the only ones to die.

No.

None of us will die for her;
Otherwise, they will be the only ones to survive.

No,

None of us will die for her;
those who do
will survive.

No.

Death has run out of time.

We will live again
after each death,

describe the clouds,
and remove the thorns
from this body.

We will live one more day
 only to spite them
forever and a day.

Let them extinguish us in the fires of our dreams
and burn us in the gardens of our lives.

From the ashes we will rise.

This country is ours even if they deny it and connive.
we own her early dreams, and for the harvest we shall strive.

Hager Ben Driss is associate professor at the University of Tunis. She teaches Anglophone literature and her research interests focus on gender and postcolonial studies. She is editor of *Knowledge: Trans/Formations* (2013) and *Women, Violence, and Resistance* (2017). She published several articles on Arabic and Tunisian literature and translated numerous Tunisian poems into English. Her work shows a keen interest in interdisciplinarity with a special focus on Mobility Studies. She has recently edited a collection of articles titled *Mobilizing Narratives: Narrating Injustices of (Im)Mobility* (2021). Ben Driss is Editor-in-Chief of the *Journal of Arts and Humanities* (Tunisia).

مطالب

سماني هجو

ما راجع أنا لي مطالب
ما راجع أنا لي مطالب
جيبوا حكومة الحكم المدني
ودم الكوز القتل الطالب
الناس مرقوا وقفوا في وش المدفع
ثوار هتفوا قالوا نحنا ما بنرجع
بناتنا قدام في كل موكب يطلع
ثوار أحرار لحكم العسكر ما بنخضع

It's really simple all we want is freedom, no violence and brutality
We fight together and we march together,
to make our dream a reality
It's really simple all we want is justice, no violence and brutality
We fight together and we march together, for peace and equality

ما راجع أنا لي مطالب
ما راجع أنا لي مطالب
جيبوا حكومة الحكم المدني
ودم الكوز القتل الطالب

مدنية
مدنية
مدنية
مدنية
مدنية
مدنية

سلمية
سلمية
سلمية

مطالب

Sammany Hajo is a Sudanese musician and beatmeaker residing in Qatar. His discography is a fusion of several genres like reggae, jazz, hip-hop, and both traditional and modern Sudanese music. In addition to producing beats, Sammany is also an instrumentalist playing the guitar and piano as his main instruments. His performance on COLORSxSTUDIOS stage debuted his singing career with his single Matalib (Demands), an anthem of honoring the Sudanese protests of 2019. The lyrics to the song are printed with the permission of the artist.

Matalib

Self-translated by Sammany Hajo

I'm not going back, I still have demands
I'm not going back, I still have demands
Give us a civilian government
And the blood of those who killed the students

The people came out to face it all
Revolutionaries chanting "we won't go back"
Our women, forever on the front lines
Revolutionary, free and ubowed by the military

It's really simple all we want is freedom, no violence and brutality
We fight together and we march together,
to make our dream a reality
It's really simple all we want is justice, no violence and brutality
We fight together and we march together, for peace and equality

I'm not going back, I still have demands
I'm not going back, I still have demands
Give us a civilian government
And the blood of those who killed the students

Civility
Civility
Civility
Civility
Civility
Civility

Peace
Peace
Peace

Demands

البحر المتوسّط

أمير حمد

كنتُ طفلاً خجولاً يغرق والده أمامه
صرخ فيّ في دوّامةٍ تشدّ روحه
من قَبّة قميصها كي أحضر النّجدة
ارتجفتُ عندما جاور اسمي في ندائه الغرق
فعاد صوته كلّ مرّةٍ خفافيش تصطدم بجسده
تجمّدتُ في مكاني ملهياً لساني بالملح على شفتي
كان أبي يجذّف بعيداً بز عانف حجّرها الزّبد
وكنتُ أرحل أبعد في شباك الصيّادين
الحالمين بالعودة إلى بيوتهم
بأسماكٍ ذهبيّةٍ تجيد رواية القصص
ثمّ عاد أبي من البحر دون مساعدتي ...
وعندما مرّ بجانبي، تفادى النّظر في عينيّ
كي يحميني من أن أبصر في وجهه الأزرق
أخطبوط خيبته.

The Mediterranean Sea

Translated by Katharine Halls

I was a timid child, his father drowning in front of him
He shouted to me, from a whirlpool tugging his soul
out of the collar of its shirt, to get help
I shook at this proximity: my own name, and drowning
His voice each time came back as bats crashing into his body
I was frozen to the spot, my tongue distracted by the salt on my lips
My father was paddling far away with fins gone stiff in the foam
And I was departing, further, in the nets of fisherpeople
who dreamt of returning home
with golden fish that tell stories
Then my father came back from the sea without my help
And when he passed me he avoided my eyes
To save me from seeing in his blue face
the octopus of his disappointment.

صلاة

امسح يا ربّ بمنديلك دخان مرايانا
أطفئ بدمعتك نار نوافذنا
لا طاقة لنا ألّا نؤمن برحمتك
الصواريخ كسّرت عظام كواكبنا
القنابل فتّت زجاج هوائنا
والشظايا تثقل عيوننا
بينما نمدّها إليك
كي تضعها على الميزان.

Ameer Hamad was born in Jerusalem. He holds a degree in computer science from Birzeit University. In 2019, he was awarded the Al-Qattan prize in two categories for his first two books: *Gigi and Ali's Rabbit*, a collection of short stories, and *I Searched for Their Keys in the Locks*, a collection of poetry.

Prayer

Lord with your cloth wipe the smoke from our mirrors
Extinguish the fire at our windows with your tears
We have no strength not to trust in your mercy
Rockets have broken the bones of our planets
Bombs have shattered the glass of our air
And the fragments lie heavy on our eyes
As we hold them out to you
That you may set them on the scales.

"Prayer" and "The Mediterranean Sea" both appeared in *Asymptote Journal*'s Translation Tuesday series.

إذا مِتّ لا تدفنوني هنا

عمر حاذق

إذا مِتّ لا تدفنوني هنا
وهاتوا السماءَ إليَّ
لألعبَ فيها مع الصبيةِ الراحلينَ؛
سنصنعُ من غيمةٍ كرةً
وسنلعبُ حتى تفيضَ على الأرضِ أحلامُنا
إذا مِتّ لا تدفنوني
لأني سأخرجُ من أي قبرٍ أريدُ
وألعبُ في نومِكم
«وأبعثرُ أحلامَكم بين صوتِ الصياحِ وصوتِ الغُنا»
دعوني، ستأتي سناجبُ تائهةٌ
وتخبِّئُ أطفالَها في جذوعي
وتأكلُ من بندقِ الكلماتِ طعامَ الهنا
سيأتي بأسماكهِ البحرُ
يبحثُ عن موجةٍ هربتْ منه ليلًا
وصارت صديقةً قلبي
ونامتْ على حِجرهِ زمنا
إذا مِتّ لا تدفنوني
لأني سأكمنُ في رحمِ الأرضِ، أنتظرُ المطر الموسميَّ
لأخرجَ من بذرتي نضرًا فاتنا
وأفتحَ وردةَ قلبي إذا عبر العاشقون أمامي
فيقطفَني مغرمٌ مثقلٌ بفراقٍ
ويسكنني وطنا
إذا مِتّ لا تدفنوني
لأني سأهربُ في جسدِ الأرضِ؛

أربطُ أشجارَكم بجذورِ كلامي
فتطعمُكم من ثماري قصائدَ مفعمةً شجنا
سأثقبُ أحواضَ أنهارِكم
وسأسرقُ من مائكم للصحارى؛
لصبّارةٍ عشقتْ نفسَها
واكتفتْ بهدوء المساءِ لتطلقَ أحلامَها سُفُنًا سفنا
إذا متّ لا تدفنوني
لأني سأبقى أنا
سأبقى أنا

Omar Hathiq is an Egyptian writer and poet. He is the author of a poetry collection entitled *I Believe the Winter's Sun* (Arabesque Publishing, 2009) and four novels in Arabic: *I Do Not Like This City* (2014), *The City's First Novelist* (2015), *The Fish's Heart* (2015), and *Life in White* (2016). He wrote his poem "If I Die, Do Not Bury Me Here" while he was imprisoned between 2013 and 2015.

If I Die, Do Not Bury Me Here

Translated by Chihab El Khachab

If I die, do not bury me here.
Bring me the sky,
So I can play with the young departed.
We'll make a ball out of clouds,
And play, until our dreams flood the earth.

If I die, do not bury me.
I will come out of any grave I like,
To play around in your sleep,
And scatter your dreams amid screams and songs.
Let me be. Lost squirrels will come
To hide their children in my stumps,
And eat my words' hazelnuts blissfully.
The sea will come, with its fish,
Looking for a wave that escaped it at night
To befriend my heart,
And nod off in its lap for a while.

If I die, do not bury me.
I will smoulder in the earth's womb, awaiting seasonal rains
To come out of my seed, a charming sprout,
And open my heart's flower were lovers to pass by;
yet an enamoured soul, weighed down by separation, picks me up,
And a homeland dwells in me.

If I die, do not bury me.
I will escape into the earth's flesh,
And tie your trees to my words' roots,
So their fruits can feed you poems briming with melancholy.
I will puncture your rivers' beds,
And steal off your water to the deserts,
To a cactus in love with itself,

And content enough with the calm night to launch its dreams, one ship after another.

If I die, do not bury me,
For I will remain.
I will remain.

Chihab El Khachab is associate professor in Visual Anthropology at the University of Oxford. He is the author of *Making Film in Egypt* (AUC Press, 2021) and *Al-Fahhama* [*The Explanation Machine*] (Diwan Publishing, 2022). He is a regular writer and translator for the Egyptian literary website, *Boring Books*.

اِحْتِفَالٌ بَهِيمِيٌّ
نوري الجراح

فَلْنَمْضِ، إِذَنْ، أَنَا وَأَنْتَ، فِي هَذَا الْمَسَاءِ الدِّمَشْقِيِّ
شَبَحَانِ غَرِيبَانِ،
يَهْبِطَانِ الْجَبَلَ؛
"هَابِيلُ" الَّذِي قُتِلَ و"قَابِيلُ" الَّذِي قَتَلْ.

وَفِي السُّوقِ الْمُسْتَقِيمِ،
حَيْثُ يَتَدَلَّى الضَّوءُ، مَعَ الْمَلَابِسِ،
بِأَبْوَابِ حَوَانِيتَ كَئِيبَةٍ،
وَتَفِرُّ الْحَمَائِمُ بِأَجْنِحَتِهَا الْمُلَطَّخَةِ بِالسُّخَامِ،
وَتَغِلُ
فِي الضَّوْءِ الْكَابِي؛
فَلْنَقِفْ هُنَاكَ وَنَتَفَرَّجْ كَمَا لَوْ كُنَّا سُيَّاحاً عَابِرِينَ
وَلَمْ نَكُنْ يَوْماً أَطْفَالَ هَذِهِ الْمَدِينَةِ،
وَلَا أَبْنَاءً لِآبَاءٍ دُفِنُوا فِي تُرَابِهَا الْأَسِيرْ.

وفِي مَدَاخِلِ الْحَوَانِيتِ،
عِنْدَ الْأَغْلَاقِ الَّتِي ضَجَّتْ،
وَالْأَقْفَالِ الَّتِي رَمَتْهَا الْأَيْدِي، سَرِيعاً، عَلَى الْأَغْلَاقِ،
قَبْلَ أَنْ يَلُوذَ أَصْحَابُهَا بِالظِّلَالِ،
جُنُودٌ بِأَسْلِحَةٍ أُوتُومَاتِيكِيَّةٍ،
سَيَصِلُونَ فِي عَرَبَاتٍ مُرَقَّطَةٍ تَغُصُّ بِالْأَعْلَامِ،
وَعَلَى أَذْرُعِهِمْ شَارَاتُ الْحَرَسِ الْجُمْهُورِي.
وَبِأَقْدَامٍ مُلَطَّخَةٍ بِالدَّمِ، يَتَرَجَّلُون،
يَتَقَدَّمُهُمْ فَتًى بِرَأْسٍ مَقْطُوعٍ،
وَمِنْ وَرَائِهِ فَقِيهٌ بِعَمَامَةٍ سَوْدَاء

قَالَ إِنَّهُ مَازَالَ يَمْشِي إِلَى دِمَشْقَ،
مُنْذُ 1400 عَامٍ،
نَازِلاً
مِنْ كَرْبَلَاءْ
وَفِي يَدَيْهِ هَذَا الرَّأْسُ النَّازِفُ.

وفِي الْمَوكِبِ، مِنَ الْوَرَاءِ،
عُصَبٌ بِصُدُورٍ مُبْهَمَةٍ لَهُمْ رُؤُوسُ أَبْقَارٍ،
وَيَنَابِيعُ الدَّمِ تَفُورُ فِي رُؤُوسِهِمُ الْمُجَرَّحَةِ بِالسَّكَاكِينِ
عَلَى مَرْأًى مِنْ دِمَشْقِيِّينَ مَبْهُوتِينَ
لَهُمْ عُيُونٌ زَاغَتْ فِي جَمَاجِمَ هَرَبَ مِنْ مَحَاجِرِهَا الضَّوْءُ
وَتَفَقَّرَتْ فِي ظُلُمَاتِهَا صُوَرٌ وَذِكْرَيَاتٌ عَنْ أَيَّامٍ أُخَرْ.

مِنْ هؤُلَاءِ اللَّاطِمِينَ صُدُورَهُمْ بِالْأَكُفِّ،
الْجَالِدِينَ ظُهُورَهُمْ بِالسَّلَاسِلِ؟!
قَالَ صَبِيٌّ،
وَهَلْ نَحْنُ فِي مَنَامٍ حَالِكٍ،
أَمْ فِي مَدِينَةٍ خَرَجَتْ مِنْ كِتَابٍ مُمَزَّقْ؟!

فَلْنَمْضِ، إِذَنْ، أَنَا وَأَنْتَ
أَنْتَ
وَأَنَا،
كَمَا يَمْضِيَ تَابُوتٌ عَلَى صَفْحَةِ نَهْرٍ
عَلَى ضِفَافٍ اقْتُلِعَتْ مِنَ الْمَجْرَى وَطَافَ بِهَا الْهَشِيمْ.

A Brutish Celebration

Translated by Allison Blecker

Let's go, then, you and I, on this Damascus evening,
two strange ghosts
descending the mountain—
Abel who was killed and Cain who did the killing.
On the Via Recta,
where light hangs from the cheerless shop doors
alongside the clothes
and pigeons flee on soot-smudged wings,
entering that dull light,
let's stand and watch, as if we were passing tourists
and had never for a day been children of this city
or the sons of fathers buried in its captive dirt.

By the shop entrances with their clanking metal gates,
the padlocks hurriedly fastened
before their owners took refuge in the shadows,
soldiers with automatic weapons arrive
in flag-draped camouflaged vehicles,
the Republican Guard insignia on their arms.
They step down with blood-smeared boots,
preceded by a boy holding a severed head,
a faqih in a black turban behind him.
He said he had been walking to Damascus for 1400 years,
coming
from Karbala
with this bleeding head in his hands.

At the back of the procession,
come fighters with bare, brutish chests,
their heads cow-like.
Springs of blood gush from the knife wounds in their heads
before the aghast residents of Damascus.

Their eyes withdraw into their skulls,
into dark sockets from which the light flees.
Images and memories from days gone by disappear into the blackness.

Who are these men who slap their chests
with the palms of their hands
and whip themselves with chains?
A boy asked,
"Are we in a dark dream
or a city torn from a tattered book?"

Let's go, then, you and I, you and I,
like a coffin on the river's surface,
between banks uprooted from a riverbed
overflowing with straw.

وِشَاحٌ أُرْجُوانِيٌّ

بِجُيُوبٍ مَلِيئَةٍ بِالْحَصَى،
أَعُودُ مِنْ هُنَاكَ:
بِالْخُضْرَةِ الَّتِي وَشَّحَتِ الْحِجَارَةَ بِالضَّوْءِ؛
بِالْأَسَى؛
بِحُطَامِ صَرَخَاتٍ؛
وَبِالصَّمْتِ بَعْدَ الْأَنْفَاسِ مَبْهُورَةً وَهَارِبَةً؛
بِالزَّبَدِ وَقَدْ تَلَاشَى؛
وَبِالْخَدَرِ الَّذِي طَافَ عَلَى نُعَاسِ الْمَاءِ؛
وَبِالْغُرُوبِ،
أَعُودُ.

بِحُزْنِ الْعَاصِفَةِ؛
وَبِالْمَوْجَةِ الَّتِي أَجْهَشَتْ.

الصَّرَخَاتُ الَّتِي أَرْسَلَهَا الْغَرْقَى وَصَلَتْ قَبْلَ مَلَابِسِهِمْ.
لَكِنَّ الْمَرَاكِبَ لَمْ تَصِلْ.

بِمُخَيِّلَةٍ أَدْمَاهَا حَجَرٌ قَدِيمٌ فِي قَاسِيُونْ،
أَعُودُ مِنْ تِلْكَ الْجَزِيرَةِ؛
وَبِقَلْبٍ حَطَّمَتْهُ مِرْسَاةٌ ثَقِيلَةٌ.

وَبِمَاذَا تُرِيدِينَ أَنْ أَعُودَ إِلَيْكِ، يَا صَغِيرَتِي
مِنْ هَذِهِ الْجَزِيرَةِ الضَّائِعَةِ الَّتِي يُسَمُّونَهَا "لِيْسْبُوسْ"،
أَبِحِلْيَةٍ مُزَيَّفَةٍ،
أَمْ بِوِشَاحٍ أَفْلَتَ مِنْ كَتِفِ فَتَاةٍ طَفَتْ عَلَى الْمَاءِ؟!

سَأَتْرُكُ مَرْكَبِيَ الْجَرِيحَ فِي عُهْدَةِ بَحَّارٍ مِنْ "كِرِيتْ"،
وأَمضِي مَعَ الْغُرُوبِ جِهَةَ الْغَرْبْ.

Nouri al-Jarrah is a Syrian poet and literary editor. He has also founded several literary magazines. Born in Damascus in 1956, he has lived in exile in London since 1986. During that time, he has published seventeen collections of poetry, including *The Boy* (1982), *Ode to a Voice* (1990), *Hamlet's Gardens* (2003), *Noah's Despair* (2014), and *No War in Troy* (2019). In his work, he draws on mythology and legends to comment on current realities—most recently, the Syrian Civil War and the resulting refugee crisis. His poems have been translated into English, Persian, French, Spanish, Italian, Greek, Turkish, and Polish. *A Boat to Lesbos*, published by Banipal Books in 2018, is the first full-length collection of his poetry to appear in English. In 2000, Nouri al-Jarrah co-founded The Centre for Arabic Geographical Literature in Abu Dhabi, which won the 2019 Sheikh Zayed Book Award for Publishing and Technology for its contribution to the preservation, distribution, and recognition of travel literature.

A Purple Scarf

With pockets full of stones,
I come back from there.
With the greenness that dresses the stones in light,
with sorrow,
with the broken pieces of screams,
and the silence after panting, fugitive breaths,
with seafoam that has already melted away,
with the numbness that floats on the somnolence of water,
and with the sunset,
I come back.

With the sadness of the storm
and the wave that breaks into tears.

The screams of the drowning arrived before their clothes.
But the boats did not arrive.

With the imagination bled by an old stone in Qasioun,
I come back from that island,
my heart dashed by a heavy anchor.

And what do you want me to bring back to you, my little girl,
from this lost island they call Lesbos—
counterfeit trinkets
or a scarf that slipped from the shoulders of a girl floating in the
water?

I'll leave my wounded boat in the care of a sailor from Crete
and go west with the sunset.

Allison Blecker received her Ph.D. from Harvard University in Near Eastern Languages and Civilizations (Arabic Literature) with a secondary field in Comparative Literature. Her dissertation, *Eco-Alterity: Writing the Environment in the Literature of North Africa and the Middle East*, is situated at the intersection of postcolonial studies, Arabic literature, and the environmental humanities. Allison is the co-translator of a collection of poetry by Nouri al-Jarrah, *A Boat to Lesbos* (2018), and her English translations of Arabic poetry have appeared in *Banipal* and *Gathering the Tide: An Anthology of Contemporary Gulf Poetry* (2011).

اعتقال قصيدة
منى كريم

عند المساء
ينفض البحر عن جسده
كل الآهات الملقاة عليه

وعند المساء
يعتقل العساكر
قصيدته من على وجنتي الشارع

. . .نطالعها:
ثمة كلمات تصرخ من الألم. . .

Arresting a Poem

Translated by Sara Elkamel

In the evening,
the ocean dusts its body
of all the moans cast into it.

And in the evening,
soldiers apprehend the ocean's poem
off the street's cheeks.

…We look it in the face:
The words wail in pain…

مدن تموت يومياً

عميقة هي الطرقات
بعد ان انتهكها الليل
والسكارى...

لن أطوي هذه الخرائط
فهذا سيؤذي أنف وطني
مما يجعله يسلب نقود الشعب
كي يقيم عملية تجميلية

كرة دم أخرى تسير
فوق جسر شرياني النحيف،
فهل ستعترضها شرطة الأمراض؟

الربيع يقع في عقلي الأيسر،
لكن ماذا عن الخريف
أطلّقني بعد أن سكن كل حياتي؟

في كل خيمة
هنالك طفل يخرج
من صحراء أمه إلى صحراء أخرى
و أخرى...

تنفس،
دع عملية حفر الرئة علينا،

تنفس،
دع النرجس يغادر روحك

أطنان من الغبار
تغطي عروقنا
لكنها ليست كما الغبار
الذي يغطي ابتساماتنا

كثير من المدن تموت يومياً
وأنا مت حينما قرر سومر
التنازل عن عرشه

آسيا
للمرة المليون تلبس معطفاً
من الحروب،
بينما أعمارنا تتحول
لقطارات هرمة.

Mona Kareem is a Bedoon writer, translator, and literary scholar. She is also an advocate of migrant rights. She was born in Kuwait to a stateless family, and this is a theme in her literary work. Her most recent publication *Femme Ghosts* is a trilingual chapbook published by Publication Studio in Fall 2019. Her work has been translated into nine languages, and appear in *Brooklyn Rail, Michigan Quarterly, Fence, Ambit, The Los Angeles Review of Books, Asymptote, Words Without Borders, Poetry International, PEN English, Modern Poetry in Translation, Two Lines,* and *Specimen.*

Cities Dying Every Day

The roads are cavernous,
ravaged by night
and the drunkards…

I will not fold these maps;
it might dent my country's nose,
prompting a raid of popular pockets
for emergency plastic surgery.

Another blood cell treads
along my artery's narrow bridge—
will the Disease Police intercept it?

Spring lies in my left brain,
but what of autumn?
It is possible it has divorced me,
after inhabiting my entire life?

Inside every tent
is a child who emerges
out of its mother's desert and into another desert
and then another…

Breathe,
leave the task of lung excavation to us.
Breathe,
let Narcissus depart your soul.

Tons of dust
shroud our veins,
but it can't compare to the dust
that shrouds our smiles.

Many cities die every day;
I myself died
when Sumer decided
to surrender the throne.

For the millionth time, Asia
dons a coat of wars—
as our lives transform
into aging trains.

كتابات عن الثورة في السودان ٢٠١٩
رانيا مأمون

وفي التشابه تذوب الملامح
وتتّسع الأحلام
بدأب النمل
نمضي قدما
تاركين عبء الأمس
في أمسه، محبوساً
بدأب النمل
نمضي
باتجاه الشمس
متماسكين
حرية .. سلام وعدالة
الثورة خيار الشعب

*

كبرت الطفلة وصغرت أحلامها
الطفلة التي حبست
في طينها
تآكلت أفراحها كلما نمت
على جسدها علامات

الأنوثة
وزحف على قلبها الصدأ
أفسد الزهر

وانتحرت البراعم
عطش لا رواء له
تتجرّع البنت ماء الملح
كل حين

ثم،
تطلق صرختها وسع المدى
وتنتظر الخلاص
السماءُ لا تجيب
البحر لا يجيب
الأرض لا تجيب
الله في عليائه
لا يجيب
ولا مجيب مطلقا

تماما
كالعدم.

ليس من سامع أبا لصراخ امرأة
حبيسةً طينها
منذ البدء إلى

المنتهى

داخل حلم
معبأ بالندى

التقينا
أزرق زاه
منبسط فينا كسماء
كنا

على ميقات الأمل ذاته
نسير على درب مليء
بالشوك والصراخ
والدماء
كنا نسير بحذر أنيق
وإن شعرنا بالتعب
نحمل بعضنا
على كتف الحبّ
نكوّن سلّماً بشرياً
أولنا يصافح الله في علياءٍ
يعودُ آخرنا مبتسماً

راضيا
كالنمل

نّدبّ على الأرض
دون ضجيج
أو صخب
حزمةُ ضوء تسافر
في الأرجاء
حرّة، بلا تخيّر
لشرق أو لغرب
أو اتجاه
الضوء أينما
حلّ أنار

والآن
تعلقّ بالقلب المرار
صرنا

صائدي نوايا
معبأة بالسم
نقتل بعضنا
قتلاً غير رحيم
ثم، ننوح على حلمنا
بعد أن
أضعناه على
قارعة الطريق

Rania Mamoun is a Sudanese writer and activist. She has published two novels in Arabic. Her short story collection, translated into English by Elisabeth Jaquette as *Thirteen Months of Sunrise* and published by Comma Press, was shortlisted for the 2020 Warwick Prize for Women in Translation. Mamoun's writing has appeared in English translation in *Mizna, Shenandoah, Banipal, Words Without Borders,* and *The Fourth River.* Her stories have appeared in translation in *The Book of Khartoum* and *Banthology,* both with Comma Press, and in *Nouvelles du Soudan* with Magellan & Cie. She has worked as an editor and contributor to arts magazines and was a presenter for the cultural program *Silicon Valley* on Sudanese television.

Selections from *Something Evergreen Called Life*

Translated by Yasmine Seale

our shadows are alike
in likeness
features melt
& dreams swell

with the diligence of ants
we go on
leaving
yesterday's burden
locked
in yesterday
weaving
strands of light into
the map of a country for everyone

with the diligence of ants
we press on
toward the sun
holding our own
determined
crying Freedom Justice Peace
Revolution is the people's choice

the girl grew up
        & narrowed her dreams
the girl trapped in clay
her joys corroding
with every sleep
on her body marks
of womanhood
on her heart
creeping rust

the flowers went to seed
the buds to suicide

thirst without relief
the girl drinks down saltwater
now and then
lets off a long-range scream
& waits for release

heaven does not answer
ocean does not answer
earth does not answer
        God on high
does not answer
no answer quite
like nothing
no one has ever heard
the scream of a woman
trapped in clay
from beginning to end

*

*(to my comrades in the resistance
committee of Wad Madani)*

in a dream
packed with dew
we met
brilliant blue
spread within us like a sky
we had
a date with hope itself
walking a trail
thick with thorns
screams & blood
we move with sleek caution
and if we get tired
we carry each other
on love's shoulder
we make a human ladder
the first of us shakes hands with God
the last of us smiles
satisfied

like ants
we creep around
without noise or
commotion
a light beam sweeps
indiscriminately east & west
directionless
irradiating where
it falls

now
bitterness clinging
to the heart
we have become
keen hunters
packed with poison
we kill each other
without mercy

then
cry over the dream
we lost on the way

Yasmine Seale's essays, poetry, visual art, and translations from Arabic and French have appeared widely. She is the author, with Robin Moger, of *Agitated Air: Poems After Ibn Arabi* (Tenement Press). Among her translations from Arabic are *The Annotated Arabian Nights* (W. W. Norton) and *Something Evergreen Called Life*, a collection of poems by Rania Mamoun (Action Books). She is currently a fellow of the Cullman Center for Scholars and Writers at the New York Public Library.

Selections from *Something Evergreen Called Life* by Rania Mamoun translated by Yasmine Seale, copyright ©2023 by Rania Mamoun. Translation copyright ©2023 by Yasmine Seale. Reprinted by permission of Action Books.

Allô le Système !
كلمات الفنانة رجاء مزيان

الطوفان راهو جاي
ناضو الزواولة.

خرجو ولاد الشعب وخرج موح مول الطابلة
à plat
الخزينة
البلاد راها عاطلة
الموس ثقب العضم وطالت بينا الطايلة
ضربتو التعليم برديتو الجيل وراها سايبة.
société عايبة
راها الثقافة غايبة

الشعب يسوطي في بوطي وانتوما حاسبين تبقو فيها خالدين،
ردمتونا فالحياة ، خليتو الموتى حاكمين،
ضحّكتو علينا قاع الاجناس وبقينا اللخرين،
مزال الناس مالجوع تموت ونتوما زاهيين بولادكم لاهيين
طلّعتو الحيط في clubs des pin وراكو مخبيين
ألف مليار فالريح مشات ومازال طامعين،
فالبقرة حالبين، قسمتو الغلة ومال البترول و راكو مكملين،
علينا عافسين واليوم مارانا ساكتين، مارانا خايفين

جمهورية...
بغيناها شعبية.
ديموقراطية ...ماهي ملكية،

الزوالي كواتو كية،
مالكادر راه تقيا ...خطونا يا باندية

اسمعني مليح يا شيات قتلك فالرابعة ...
غير نساني في خبزك أنا ماني طامعة،

كليتو البلاد يا الحركى واليوم راهي حابسة،
و بغيتو تزيدو الخامسة،
حسبتو الشبيبة ناعسة
خرجنا للزنقة نقولو خلاص وراكم خايفين،
للفوضى حابين، خسرتو وربحنا هاد المرة وماكم طالقين،
راكم حالفين، تخلو البلاد في محنة كحلة وتبدو هاربين،
رانا شافيين،
مارانا ناسيين، مارانا مسامحين
خدعتو التاريخ و الثورة ومازال كاين شاهدين، وعليكم حاقدين
ان شالله ترجع هاذ البلاد و تعودو خايبين

جمهورية ...
بغيناها شعبية...
ديموقراطية ...ماهي ملكية،

الزوالي كواتو كية،
مالكادر راه تقيا ...خطونا يا باندية

جمهورية ...
بغيناها شعبية...
ديموقراطية ...ماهي ملكية،

الزوالي كواتو كية،
مالكادر راه تقيا ...خطونا يا باندية.

Raja Meziane is an Algerian singer, songwriter, lawyer, and activist. She was born in 1988 in northwestern Algeria. Her song "Allô le Système !" is an anthem of the Algerian protests of 2019. After the release of her song, she was listed as one of BBC's 100 most influential women of the year in 2019. The lyrics to her song are printed with permission from the artist and her team.

Allô le Système !

Self-translated by Raja Meziane

The flood is at your door
The crowd is coming out
Young, old, jobless, and even the street hustlers
The coffers are empty
The country is bankrupt
The knife pierced the marrow, and it has been for too long
You've crushed education, a whole generation is lost
The society is blocked
The culture absent

People leave the country in makeshift boats
You think you're eternal
You've buried us alive and left the dead in power
We've become the laughingstock of all
People are starving and you're partying,
you care for no one but your kids
Hidden behind your walls, you're frightened.
1000 billion dollars gone up in smoke and you still want more
You're milking the cow for all its worth
Oil rents well-kept and shared among you
And again, you crush us
Today we are no longer silent
We are no longer afraid.

We want a republic
A people's democracy, not a monarchy
People have suffered enough
They are sick of you
We are the flood
You best leave us alone, you thugs

We want a republic
A people's democracy, not a monarchy

People have suffered enough
They are sick of you
We are the flood
You best leave us alone, you thugs.

Listen to me, you puppet of this system
I told you in the fourth mandate
Just leave me alone, I will not be a part of it
You took it all and there is not much left to take
But you still want a fifth round
You thought the youth was asleep
Now we are in the streets to say stop and you are shaking
You hope for chaos
But this time we win, you lose
But you will never quit
You vowed to leave the country to fire and blood and run away
We know you well
We have not forgotten
We will not forgive
You have corrupted history and betrayed the revolution
The witnesses are still there and they despise you

Inshallah this country will recover
and you will get what you deserve

We want a republic
A people's democracy, not a monarchy
People have suffered enough
They are sick of you
We are the flood
You best leave us alone, you thugs

We want a republic
A people's democracy, not a monarchy
People have suffered enough
They are sick of you
We are the flood
You best leave us alone, you thugs

موطني
إبراهيم طوقان

موطني... موطني
الجلالُ والجمالُ والسناءُ والبهاءُ
في رُباكْ... في رُباكْ

والحياةُ والنجاةُ والهناءُ والرجاءُ
في هواك... في هواك
هل أراكْ... هل أراكْ
سالماً منعَّماً وغانماً مكرَّماً؟
هل أراكْ... في علاكْ
تبلغ السِّماكْ؟... تبلغ السِّماكْ؟

موطني... موطني..
موطني.. موطني
الشبابُ لن يكلَّ همُّه أن تستقلَّ أو يبيدْ
نستقي من الـردى ولن نكون للعدى
كالعبيد... كالعبيد

لا نريدْ... لا نريدْ.. ذلَّنا المؤبَّدا
وعيشَنا المنكَّدا لا نريدْ... بل نُعيدْ
مجدَنا التليدْ... مجدَنا التليدْ

موطني... موطني..
موطني.. موطني
الحسامُ واليَراعُ لا الكلامُ والنزاعُ
رمزُنا... رمزُنا
مجدُنا وعهدُنا وواجبٌ من الوَفا

يهزّنا... يهزّنا
..عزُّنا... عزُّنا
غايةٌ تُشرِّفُ ورايةٌ تُرفرفُ
يا هَناكْ في عُلاكْ
قاهراً عِداكْ... قاهراً عِداكْ
موطني... موطني

Ibrahim Tuqan was a Palestinian Nationalist poet whose work spoke to Arab unity during their revolt against the British mandate. Tuqan was born in Nablus, Palestine. He was the brother of poet Fadwa Tuqan and tutored and influenced her to write poetry. His poem "Mawtini" was adopted as the national anthem of several Arab states and continues to be popular today.

My Homeland

Translated by Maha Salah

O Homeland, my dear homeland,
Majesty, beauty, magnificence, and grace
Lie in your peaks

A dignified life, salvation, joy, and hope
Move in your breeze.
Will I ever see you,
Safely at peace and triumphantly victorious?
Will I see you, at your peak
Reaching the highest heavens

O Homeland, my dear homeland
O Homeland, my dear homeland,
The youth will never grow weary, they yearn for your liberty
Or martyrdom, death, and sacrifice.
We would prefer death over serving our enemies,
as slaves.

We refuse, we simply refuse
Eternal degradation and bleak lives
We refuse it and will restore
Our legendary glory,
O Homeland, my dear homeland

O Homeland, my dear homeland,
Swords and pens, not words and war
Represent us and are our symbols,
Our glory and promise, our devotion to our duty
Inspire us
Our pride, our pride
Is our honorable mission and our allegiance to your waving banner,

May we rejoice in your transcendence
As you prevail over your enemies
O Homeland, my dear homeland

Maha Salah is a Palestinian-American translator and interpreter. She has worked for a London-based media organization as a translator, interpreter, food blogger, and regular contributor. Her translation work in English and Arabic has appeared in *Al-Jazeera*, *The Guardian*, and elsewhere. She has also interpreted at several venues. She is currently based in Doha, Qatar with her husband and three children.

FRENCH

Je te dis printemps

Tahar Bekri

Je te dis printemps
La couleur de l'hiver
C'est le gel tardif qui retient ton éclosion
Ou le désert ensablé dans les tempêtes
Qui enchaîne tes collines aux incendies

Un cri tombe un autre s'élève les murs en pleurs
Que de linceuls couvrent
Tes cerisiers empaillés
Sous la rosée
Mes paupières essuyant tant de poussière

Je te dis printemps

Les revers de l'hiver
La mer se jetant dans les bras des rivières

Cette lueur déchirée par les cornes de la brume
Les mensonges comme des montures
Pour les grands naufrages

Dans la fissure béante
Serpents scorpions à ciel ouvert

Je te dis printemps

Le cercle des funambules
Sur les cordes du vertige
Acrobates des bûchers
Cyclopes ressuscités

Dans la chevauchée des macchabées
Aujourd'hui comme hier

Ce n'est pas un merle qui chante sur la branche
Mais une tulipe noire qui hante ma demeure

I Tell You Spring

Translated by Khalid Lyamlahy

I tell you spring
The winter's color
Is the belated frost that holds your blooming
Or the desert silted up in storms
That chains your hills to fire

One cry falls another rises walls in tears
So many shrouds cover
Your embalmed cherry trees
Under the dew
I blink to wipe away so much dust

I tell you spring

The winter's setbacks
The sea flowing into the rivers' arms

This gleam torn by misty horns
Lies are like mounts
For major wrecks

In the gaping crack
Open-air snakes and scorpions

I tell you spring
The circle of tightrope walkers
On vertigo's ropes
Pyre acrobats
Resurrected Cyclopes
In the cavalcade of corpses
Today as yesterday

It is not a blackbird branch-singing
But a black tulip haunting my home

Mûrier dans le printemps arabe

D'étranges corneilles
Ont volé ta floraison
L'ombre confondue avec le soleil

Il est loin le chant que j'ai élevé
Parmi tes solennels feuillages
La Nuit lourde de son sommeil

Il est loin le vent qui apportait
Mon pollen à tes bourgeons alertes
Abri des rouges-gorges au réveil

Dis mûrier
C'est de soie merveille qu'il s'agit
Ou de vers qui rongent la saison

Dis mûrier
C'est d'aube écarlate que tu te nourris
Ou de chenilles dévorant tous ces papillons

A Mulberry Tree in the Arab Spring

Strange crows
Stole your blossoming
Confused shadows with sun

Gone is the song I once raised
Among your solemn leaves
The heavily sleeping Night

Gone is the wind that used to bring
My pollen to your lively buds
A shelter for robins on waking

Tell me mulberry tree
Is this about marvellous silk
Or worms gnawing the season

Tell me mulberry tree
Do you subsist on scarlet dawn
Or caterpillars, devouring not-yet butterflies

L'épopée des nus

Ils arrivèrent sombres et nus
Aux portes des villes repues
Le ciel sourd aux étoiles
Les mouettes pour seules compagnies
Et des rêves comme des mirages
Remplis d'or et de défi
Ils échouèrent sur le large des côtes
Où le partage a couleur d'oubli
Où ton nom
Déroule sa houle
Dans les affres du sable enseveli
O vieil océan
Quel gouvernail pour attendrir les vagues
Quelle mer pour recevoir les fleuves et les rivières
Mêler sel et douce source
Sans bois morts
Sans eaux troubles
Mais le limon
Fertile et fraternel

The Epic of the Naked

They arrived dark and naked
At the gates of replete cities
The sky deaf to its stars
Seagulls their only companions
And dreams like mirages
Filled with gold and defiance
They washed up off the coasts
Where sharing has the color of oblivion
Where your name
Unrolls its swell
Into the throes of buried sand
O old ocean
Which rudder can soften your waves
Which sea can host such rivers and streams
Mix salt with sweet source
No dead wood
No troubled waters
Only the silt
Fertile and fraternal

Lampedusa

Si ta main se ferme comme la pierre
Si ton olivier fait peur aux oiseaux
Si ta porte est un rideau de fer
Si ta cloche est sourde aux cris de la mer
Si l'horizon remplit ton cœur d'épouvantails
Si ta carabine tire sur les radeaux de fortune

Comment peux-tu honorer la terre ?

Si ton cactus ne sait donner que des épines
Si ton muret est une frontière pour les rapaces
Si ta vigne ne partage pas ses raisins
Si ton rivage vomit les corps anonymes
Si ton cimetière ne vaut pas une prière
Si ton rêve est une mouette empaillée

Comment peux-tu aimer la liberté ?

Tahar Bekri was born in 1951 in Gabès, Tunisia. A prolific poet, he writes in both French and Arabic. He has lived in Paris since 1976 and published more than thirty titles including poetry, essays, and art books. His poetry was translated into several languages and has been the object of various academic studies and artistic creations. Bekri is also an honorary lecturer at the Université Paris-Nanterre. He was awarded the "Prix international de Littérature francophone – Benjamin Fondane" in 2018 and the "Prix du Rayonnement de la langue et de la littérature françaises de l'Académie Française" in 2019. His most recent publications include *Chants pour la Tunisie* (with paintings by Annick Le Thoër) (Al Manar, 2023), *Par-delà les lueurs* (with paintings by Annick Le Thoër), *Désert du crépuscule* (Al Manar, 2018).

Lampedusa

If your hand closes like stone
If your olive tree scares birds
If your door is an iron curtain
If your bell is deaf to the cries of the sea
If the horizon fills your heart with scarecrows
If your rifle fires on makeshift rafts

How can you honor the earth?

If your cactus can only give thorns
If your low wall is a border for raptors
If your vineyard withholds its grapes
If your shore expels anonymous bodies
If your cemetery is not worth a prayer
If your dream is an embalmed seagull

How can you love freedom?

Khalid Lyamlahy is assistant professor of French and Francophone Studies at the University of Chicago where he teaches North African literature. He is the co-editor, with Jane Hiddleston, of *Abdelkébir Khatibi: Postcolonialism, Transnationalism, and Culture in the Maghreb and Beyond* (Liverpool University Press, 2020), and has written the preface to the complete poetic work of Moroccan poet Abdellatif Laâbi (Éditions du Sirocco, 2018).

In addition to academic work, he is the author of two novels, *Un roman étranger* (2017) and *Évocation d'un mémorial à Venise* (2023), both published by Éditions Présence Africaine. He is also the co-author, with Rym Khene, of a chapbook of poetry and photography, *J'ai rencontré un cheval de mer* (Éditions La place, 2022), and has translated Felwine Sarr's *Habiter le monde : essai de politique relationnelle* into Arabic (Kulte Éditions, 2022).

Translator's note: The above poems by Tunisian poet Tahar Bekri are from his collection *Mûrier triste dans le printemps arabe* [*A Sad Mulberry Tree in the Arab Spring*] published by Al Manar in France in 2016. The first two deal with the aftermath of the so-called "Arab Spring", the wave of popular protests that erupted in Tunisia in December 2010 and spread to the rest of the Arab world. The following two poems evoke the tragedy of migrants who die trying to cross the Mediterranean or, when they reach Europe's southern shores, are met with hostility and intolerance. Bekri's poetry, at once lucid and melancholic, testifies to an ongoing quest for dignity and freedom, often threatened by the return of violence but always open to the regenerative power of writing. Translating poetry is both a huge challenge and a delightful experience. I would like to thank Tahar Bekri and his publisher Alain Gorius from Al Manar for their kind permission. My special thanks go to my friend, scholar and poet Lacey Jones for her extremely valuable comments and suggestions.

L'Analphabète

Ahmed Bouanani

Si tu veux...
Je me dis chaque jour : si tu veux revoir les chiens noirs de ton enfance, fais-toi une raison. Jette tes cheveux dans la rivière de mensonge, plonge, plonge plus profondément encore dans le sang de la démence. Que t'importe les masques, mais fais-toi une raison et meurs s'il le faut parmi les têtes chauves, les gosses des bidonvilles mangeurs de sauterelles et de lunes chaudes, et les chiens noirs que s'ébattent dans les dépotoirs des faubourgs.

En ce temps-là,
il pleuvait des saisons des couleurs, il pleuvait de la lune des dragons légendaires. Le ciel bienfaiteur s'ouvrait sur des cavaliers blancs. Même que sur les terrasses de Casablanca chantaient des vieilles femmes coquettes.

Une nuit,
un enfant attira la lune dans un guet-apens.
Dix ans plus tard, il la retrouva vieille et toute pâle, plus vieille encore que les vieilles femmes sans miroirs, les grands-mères moustachues palabrant comme la mauvaise pluie.
Alors,
il comprit que les saisons de couleurs étaient une invention des ancêtres.
Ce fut
la mort des arbres, la mort des géants. Ghalia bent el Mansour ne vivait pas au-delà des sept mers dans un chateau d'émeraudes sur le dos des aigles. Il la rencontra au bidonville de Ben M'Sik si ce n'est pas aux Carrières Centrales, près des baraques foraines. Elle portait des chaussures en plastique et elle se prostituait avec le réparateur de bicyclettes.
Il n'y avait plus qu'à claquer les portes du ciel.
Alors, les mains en flammes, je recommençai les soleils.

Mon mal est un monde barbare qui se veut sans arithmétiques ni calculs.

Je drape les égouts et les dépotoirs,
j'appelle amis tous les chiens noirs, tous les cafards qui escaladent mes rêves de fou.
Pardonnez-moi et que le diable vous emporte ! Aimez, admirez, détestez ce que bon vous semble. Mon usine est sans robots, mes machines sont en grève, les vagues de mon océan parlent un langage qui n'est pas le vôtre.
Pardonnez-moi et que le diable vous emporte. Je suis mort et vous m'accusez de vivre, je fume des cigarettes de second ordre et vous m'accusez de brûler des fermes féodales.
Écoutez, écoutez-moi.
Par quelle loi est-il permis au coq de voler plus haut que l'aigle ?
En rêve le poisson voudrait sauter jusqu'au septième ciel.
J'ai bâti des terrasses et des villes entières. Casablanca vivait sous la bombe américaine. Ma tante tremblait dans les escaliers et il lui semblait voir le ciel s'ouvrir par le ventre. Mon frère M'hammed avec la flamme d'une bougie faisait danser Charlot et Dick Tracy. Ma mère...
Dois-je vraiment revenir à la maison aux persiennes ?
Les escaliers envahis par une armée de rats, la femme nue aux mains de sorcelleries, Allal violant Milouda dans une mare de sang, et les Sénégalais coupant son sexe à un boucher du Derb Al Kabir...
Dois-je vraiment revenir à la maison aux persinennes ?
La sentinelle se lave les pieds dans tes larmes. Ton rêve le plus aimé bascule dans le monde barbare du jour et de la lune.
Tu ne tiens pas debout.
Tes équations dans les poches,
le monde sur les cornes du taureau,
le poisson dans le nuage,
le nuage dans la goutte d'eau,
et la goutte d'eau contenant l'infini.
Les murs du ciel saignent par tous les pores.
Des chiens entonnent un chant barbare. Un chant kabyle ou une légende targuie, peut-être est-ce tout simplement un conte, et ce conte s'achève en tombant dans le ruisseau.

Il met des sandales en papier,
sort dans la rue,
regarde ses pieds
      et trouve
           qu'il marche
                pieds nus.
Les murs du ciel saignent par tous les pores.
Le vent, les nuages, la terre et la forêt, les hommes devenus chansons populaires…
Derrière le soleil,
des officiers
creusent
des tombes.
Un homme est mort, une balle de 7,65 dans la nuque. Et puis, voici une vieille qui se lamente, en voici une autre qui raconte des histoires de miel et de lait où il est question d'un fils de bûcheron teigneux qui gagne la moitié d'un royaume en décapitant les sept têtes d'un ghoule…
Le vent fou de joie se lève soudain sur ses genoux,
éteint le feu sous la marmite,
dégringole les escaliers et
s'en va s'amuser sur les pavés de la rue de Monastir en racontant les mêmes histoires lubriques aux fenêtres des alentours. Et la poitrine pleine, et les yeux en feu, les maisons et les terrasses, et même le soleil surgi d'un silo vide franchissent le plafond jusqu'à mon lit.
Mes cheveux
      ou mes mains
           retrouvent
                l'usage de la parole.
De ce que j'ai le plus aimé
je veux préserver la mémoire intacte.
les lieux — les noms — les gestes — nos voix
Un chant est né. Était-ce un chant ?
De ce que j'ai le plus aimé
je veux préserver la mémoire intacte. Mais, soudain, voilà :
les lieux se confondent avec d'autres lieux, les noms glissent un à

un dans la mort.
Une colline bleue a parlé. Où donc était-ce ?
Un chant est né. Ma mémoire se réveille, mes pas ne connaissent plus les chemins, mes yeux ne connaissent plus la maison ni les terrasses, la maison où vivaient autrefois des fleurs et un chapelet de la Kaaba. Le monde, pas plus grand qu'un papier journal. Dans ce monde, il n'y a pas de vent fou ni de maisons qui dansent,
il y a
      derrière le soleil
            des officiers
                  creusant
                        des tombes,

et
dans le silence
le fracas des pelles
remplace le chant.
    Victor Hugo buvait dans un crâne à la santé des barricades. Maiakovski, lui, désarçonnait les nuages dans les villes radiophoniques. Il fallait chercher la flûte de vertèbres aux cimetières du futur. Aujourd'hui, il me faut désamorcer les chants d'amour, les papillons fumant la pipe, les fleurs ont la peau du loup, les innocents oiseaux se soûlent à la bière, il en est même quelques-uns qui cachent un revolver ou un couteau. Mon cœur a loué une garçonnière au bout de mes jambes…
Allons,
réveillez-vous, les hommes.
Des enfants du soleil en sortira-t-il encore
des balayeurs et des mendiants ?
Où donc est passé celui-là qui faisait trembler les morts dans les campagnes ? et celui-là qui brisait un pain de sucre en pliant un bras ? et celui-là qui disparaissait par les bouches d'égoûts après avoir à lui tout seul renversé un bataillon de jeeps et de camions ?
Toutes les mémoires sont ouvertes,

mais le vent a emporté les paroles,
mais les ruisseaux ont emporté les paroles.
Il nous reste des paroles étranges

un alphabet étrange
      qui s'étonnerait à la vue d'une chamelle.
L'aède s'est tu.
Pour s'abriter de la pluie, Mririda s'est jetée dans le ruisseau.
A l'école on mange de l'avoine.
La phrase secrète ne délivre plus.
Cet enfant ne guérira-t-il jamais ? Prépare-lui ma sœur la recette que je t'ai indiquée, et n'oublie pas d'écraser l'oiseau dans le mortier, c'est bon pour la santé ! Mais enfin, de quoi souffre-t-il ? Vois-tu, mon père à moi n'a pas fait la guerre. Il a hérité de ses ancêtres un coffre plein de livres et de manuscrits. Il passait des soirées entières à les lire. Une fois, il s'endormit, et à son réveil, il devint fou. Quinze jours durant, il eut l'impression de vivre dans un puits très très profond. Il creusait, creusait furieusement, mais il ne parvenait pas à atteindre la nappe d'eau. Il eut grande soif. Le seizième jour, ma mère lui fit faire un talisman coûteux qui le rendit à la raison. Seulement, depuis ce jour, il était devenu analphabète. Il ne savait même plus écrire son nom. Quand il retrouva le coffre, il prit une hache et le réduisit en morceaux. Ma mère s'en servit pour faire cuire la tête du mouton de **l'Aïd El Kabir**.
Aujourd'hui encore, lorsque je demande à mon père où sont passés les livres et les manuscrits, il me regarde très longuement et me répond :
Je crois, je crois bien que je les ai laisés au fond du puits.

                                                                                      (1967)

The Illiterate Man

Translated by Emma Ramadan

If you want…
I tell myself each day: If you want to see the black dogs of your childhood again, give yourself a reason. Throw your hair into the river of lies, plunge, plunge further still into the blood of insanity. Who cares about the masks, but accept it and die if necessary among the bald heads, the slum kids who eat grasshoppers and hot moons, and the black dogs that play in the garbage dumps of the suburbs.
In those days,
the seasons rained colors, the moon rained legendary dragons. The beneficent sky opened onto white horsemen. Just as the coquettish old women sang over the terraces of Casablanca.
One night,
a child lured the moon into a trap.
Ten years later he found it again, old and all pale, even older than the old women without mirrors, the mustachioed grandmothers arguing endlessly like rank rain.
Then,
he understood that the seasons of colors were an invention of the ancestors.
It was
the death of trees, the death of giants. Ghalia bent el Mansour didn't live beyond the seven seas in an emerald castle on the backs of the eagles. He met her in the neighborhood of Ben M'sik or else at the Carrières Centrales, near the fairground kiosks. She wore plastic shoes and prostituted herself with the bicycle repairman. There was nothing left to do but slam the doors to the sky.
Then, hands ablaze, I restarted the suns.

My illness is a savage world that aims to be without arithmetic or calculations.
I cover the sewers and the garbage dumps.

All the black dogs, all the cockroaches that crawl through my deranged dreams I call friends.
Forgive me and to the devil with you! Love, admire, detest as you see fit.

My factory has no robots, my machines are on strike, the waves of my ocean speak a language that is not yours.
Forgive me and to the devil with you. I am dead and you accuse me of living, I smoke second-rate cigarettes and you accuse me of burning feudal farms.
Listen, listen to me.
According to what law can the chicken fly higher than the eagle?
In its dreams the fish tries to leap to the seventh heaven.
I built terraces and entire cities. Casablanca lived under the American bomb. My aunt trembled in the stairs and thought she saw the sky open by its stomach. My brother M'hammed made Charlot and Dick Tracy dance with the flame of a candle. My mother . . .
Must I really go back to the house of the shutters?
The stairs infested with an army of rats, the naked woman with sorceress hands, Allal raping Milouda in a pool of blood, and the Senegalese man cutting off his penis at a butcher's in Derb Al Kabir . . .
Must I really go back to the house of the shutters?
The sentinel washes his feet with your tears. Your dearest dream topples over in the savage world of daylight and moon.
You do not stand up.
Your equations in your pockets,
the world on the horns of the ox,
the fish in the cloud,
the cloud in the drop of water,
and the drop of water containing infinity.
The walls of the sky bleed from every pore.
The dogs burst into a savage song. A Kabylian song or a Targuie legend, perhaps it's simply a tale, and this tale ends by falling into the stream.

He puts on paper sandals,
goes out into the street,
looks at his feet
     and finds
          that he's walking
               barefoot.
The walls of the sky bleed from every pore.
The wind, the clouds, the land and the forest, the men turned into
traditional songs...
Behind the sun,
the officers
dig
the tombs.
A man is dead, a 7.65mm bullet to the neck. And there is an old
woman whining, there is another recounting stories of milk and
honey, one about the son of a nasty lumberjack who wins half a
kingdom by decapitating a ghoul's seven heads...
The thrilled wind suddenly rises to its knees,
extinguishes the fire under the pot,
tumbles down the stairs and
goes to play on the cobblestones of rue de Monastir telling the
same lewd stories to the surrounding windows. My chest full, my
eyes on fire, the houses and the terraces and even the sun, emerged
from an empty silo, break through the ceiling all the way to
my bed.
My hair
     or my hands
          rediscover
               the use of speech.
For the things I loved the most
I want to keep my memory intact...
The places—the names—the actions—our voices.
A song is born. Was it a song?
For the things I loved the most
I want to keep my memory intact. But, suddenly,

it happens:
Places get confused with other places, names slip one by one to their deaths.
A blue hill spoke. Where was it?
A song is born. My memory wakes up, my steps no longer know the paths, my eyes no longer know the house or the terraces, the house in former days filled with flowers and a rosary from the Kaaba. The world, no bigger than a newspaper. In this world, there is no delirious wind or dancing houses
behind the sun
    there are
        officers
            digging
                tombs
and
in the silence
the roar of shovels
replaces the song.
Victor Hugo drank from a skull to the health of the barricades. Mayakovsky disrupted the clouds in the radio cities. We had to search for the flute of vertebrae in the cemeteries of the future. Today, I must defuse the love songs, the butterflies smoke pipes, the flowers have wolf's skin, the innocent birds get drunk on beer, some even hide a revolver or a knife. My heart rented a bachelor pad between my legs.
Let's go,
wake up, men.
Will the children of the sun still end up as
sweepers and beggars?
Where did he go, the man that made the dead in the countryside tremble? and the man who, bending his arm, shattered a sugarloaf? and the man who disappeared by the entrance to the sewers after overturning a battalion of trucks and jeeps?
All the memories are open,
but the wind has swept away the words,

but the streams have swept away the words.
We are left with
      strange words
a strange alphabet
          that would be astonished to see a camel.

The bard went quiet.
To take shelter from the rain, Mririda threw herself into the stream.
At school, we eat oats.
The secret password no longer sets you free.
Will that child never recover? My sister, prepare him the recipe I mentioned, and don't forget to crush the bird in the mortar, it's good for the health! But really, what does he suffer from?
You see, my father wasn't in the war. He inherited from his ancestors a trunk full of books and manuscripts. He spent entire nights reading them. Once, he fell asleep, and when he woke up, he went crazy. For fifteen days, he believed he was living in a very, very deep well. He furiously dug and dug, but never managed to reach groundwater. He was extremely thirsty. On the sixteenth day, my mother made a precious talisman for him that restored his reason. Except, that day, he became illiterate. He didn't even know how to write his name. When he found the trunk again, he took an ax and smashed it to pieces. My mother used the wood to cook the head of the sheep for Eid al-Adha, the Sacrifice Feast.
To this day, when I ask my father what happened to the books and the manuscripts, he looks at me for a long time and says:
I believe, I do believe that I left them at the bottom of the well.

                                              (1967)

Aux poètes prisonniers

Malheur à qui porta la main
sur les poètes prisonniers
Heureux les poètes prisonniers
mes copains
intacts en ce règne
Au fond de moi chaque jour
j'entends se répercuter les cadenas qui vous
retiennent
Au fond de moi dans mon sang
immenses vigilents vous avez réussi
à percer des labyrinthes sous les remparts
Mais
en voici un (inutile de te nommer)
maigre hirsute un ciel dans les yeux
et des oiseaux clandestins
Dès que les gardiens tournent le dos
il vole
il vient nous saluer
et très souvent malgré la fatigue
il traverse la mer
Les oiseaux te connaissent
Il y a des lambeaux de nuage sur ta barbe
essuie-les avant de regagner les murs
Heureux mes copains
les poètes prisonniers
car sous la terre ils voient
plus loin que nous
Nul tombeau ne peut les contenir.

Ahmed Bouanani was born in Casablanca. When Bouanani was sixteen, during the final days of the colonial era, his father, a police officer, was assassinated—a tragedy that the artist returned to in his work for the rest of his life. Bouanani studied film at the Institut des hautes études cinématogrpahiques (IDHEC) in Paris for three years before returning to Morocco and went on to direct several classics of North African cinema. Most of his movies have their genesis in poems, and he published three collections during his lifetime, as well as a novel, *The Hospital*.

To the Poet Prisoners

Misfortune to he who laid a hand
on the poet prisoners
Happy are the poet prisoners
my friends
intact in this kingdom
Inside me each day
I hear the echo of the padlocks
that hold you back
Inside me in my blood
you immense vigilant have succeeded
in penetrating the labyrinths under the ramparts
But
here's one now (no use naming you)
meager disheveled a sky in your eyes
and secret birds
As soon as the guards turn their backs
he flies
he comes to greet us
and often despite the fatigue
he crosses the sea
The birds know you
There are shreds of cloud in your beard
wipe them off before going back to the walls
Happy are my friends
the poet prisoners
for beneath the earth they see
much further than us
No tombstone can contain them.

Emma Ramadan is a French-English literary translator of poetry and prose from France, North Africa, and the Middle East. She is the recipient of a Fulbright, two NEA Translation Fellowships, the 2018 Albertine Prize, and the 2021 PEN Translation Prize.

"The Illiterate Man" and "To the Poet Prisoners," by Ahmed Bouanani, translated by Emma Ramadan, from The Shutters, copyright ©1980, 1989 by Ahmed Bouanani. Copyright © 2018 by Touda Bouanani. Translation copyright © 2018 by Emma Ramadan. Reprinted by permission of New Directions Publishing Corp.

Le 17 octobre

Hadrien Bureau et Tracy Nehmé

Une forêt de cèdres pousse dans la rue
Sur la place, un immense poing au ciel tendu
Devant moi, des nuages puissants de drapeaux
Qui se faufilent à travers tous les barreaux.

La révolution commence. C'est la fête.
On marche avec des rêves vibrants plein la tête
Il faut se pincer vraiment très fort pour y croire
Tout paraissait si terne, si gris et si noir.

Le changement, on en parlait qu'à son miroir
Et seulement la nuit bien cachés dans le noir
Mais soudain, pris de folie, le peuple est sorti
Comme un printemps joyeux qui bondit de son lit

L'air est plein de rires, de chants, de joie, de cris
On refait le monde autant le jour que la nuit
Le temps s'arrête sous les tentes élevées
Où des étoiles fleurissent en liberté

Ce bonheur est un sentiment indescriptible
Certains murmurent que tout est enfin possible
Pour la première fois, peut-être, le Liban
N'est plus que cette foule unie en mouvement

De vieilles grand-mères rayonnent et puis dansent
Autour d'enfants encore gavés d'innocence
Des artistes dessinent la révolte aux murs
Et le vieux monde s'effraie de nos peintures.

Un pays. Sa force. C'est naïf, mais c'est beau.
Une voix mêlée à des millions d'échos.

Pour de bon, on se dit que la guerre est passée
Pour de bon, on se dit qu'un peuple s'est levé.

Soudain, je te vois. Je peine à te reconnaitre
Tu as changé. J'ai devant moi un nouvel être
Tu rayonnes : tu es plus grand et plus fier
Tu renais pour voir la fin du monde d'hier
Tu cours vers moi avec ton immense sourire
Dans tes bras je crois reconnaitre l'avenir
On se tient tous les trois : le bonheur, toi et moi
C'est fou ! C'est bien là ? Personne vraiment n'y croit !

Même dans tous nos rêves les plus insensés
Même dans ce pays où règne pourtant l'été
Même avec nos mains et tout l'ocre de la terre
Même avec nos coeurs, nos bruits et nos prières.

Mais nous sommes debout et nous sommes tous dignes.
Nous avons découvert une chose sublime
Une vérité profonde, vaste et puissante
Nous sommes Libanais. Une lumière combattante.

C'est étrange. Les visages sont différents.
On se sent tous aussi libres que l'océan
On se montre au grand jour, on ne se cache plus
Regardez. Nous sommes des astres aux mains nus.

J'ai peur. J'ai peur qu'après la joie vienne l'orage
Et qu'il ne reste à la fin qu'un sombre mirage.
Ce serait si injuste d'étouffer ainsi
Notre cri, notre idéal sorti de l'oubli

Aujourd'hui, les rues sont de nouveau désertes
Pour un temps, le régime a conservé sa tête
Et le peuple est rentré chez lui triste et amer
Et dans nos cœurs, c'est le silence de la mer.

Mais il faut le dire bien haut. Pour qu'ils le sachent.
Nous avons marqué notre Histoire d'une tâche
Un peuple muet n'est un pas peuple qui dort
Aussi longue que soit la nuit, viendra l'aurore

Ce que nous défendons est toujours immortel
Un jour, il suffira d'une seule étincelle
Et nous verrons nos balcons et nos cœurs fleurir
D'un seul et vieux drapeau qui ne saurait mourir.

Hadrien Bureau is a former student of the École Normale Supérieure, and associate professor of Economics and Management in Paris. Passionate about political rhetoric, he worked with several politicians as a speech writer (ministerial office, office of the President of the National Assembly, presidential campaign) as well as in a corporate context. He also offers trainings in speech production and political communication.

Tracy Nehmé's mission is to find new ways to increase citizens' engagement and improve democratic processes. She founded Citizens & Politics in 2017, a civic education NGO aiming at bringing back politics to the people. She holds a BA in Electrical and Computer Engineering and an MA in Public Policy and International Affairs from the American University of Beirut. She worked in various fields including corporate social responsibility, digital communication, and non-profit project management.

October 17th

Self-translated by Hadrien Bureau and Tracy Nehmé

A forest of cedars is growing across the street
In the square, a huge fist is stretched to the sky
Facing me are clouds of flags
That sneak through all the bars.

The revolution starts. It's a celebration.
We walk with vibrant dreams in our heads
We have to pinch ourselves hard to believe it
Everything seemed so dull, so grey and so black.

We only spoke to our mirror about change
And only at night, well hidden in the dark
Suddenly, taken by madness, the people stepped out
Like a joyful spring that leaps from its bed

The air is full of laughter, songs, joy, and cries
We remake the world by day and by night
Time stands still under the tents raised up high
Where stars bloom in freedom.

This happiness is an indescribable feeling
Some whisper that everything is finally possible
For the first time ever, Lebanon
Becomes a united crowd in motion.

Grandmothers are beaming and dancing
Around children still full of innocence
Artists draw the revolt on the walls
And the old world is afraid of our paintings.

A country. Its strength. Naive but beautiful.
A voice mixed with millions of echoes.

For real, we say to ourselves that this time the war is over
For real, we say to ourselves that our people have risen.

Suddenly, I see you. I hardly recognise you
You have changed. I have before me a new being
You're shining: you look taller and prouder
You are reborn to see the end of yesterday's world

You run towards me with your huge smile
In your arms I think I recognise the future
The three of us are standing together: happiness, you and I
It's crazy! Is it really here? Its so hard to believe!

Even in our craziest dreams
Even in this country where summer reigns
Even with our hands and all the ochre of the earth
Even with our hearts, our screams and our prayers

But we are standing proud and we are deserving of this.
We have discovered a sublime thing
A deep, vast and powerful truth
We are Lebanese. A fighting light.

It is strange. The faces look different.
We all feel as free as the ocean
We show ourselves in the open, we don't hide anymore
Look at us. We are stars with bare hands.

I am afraid. I'm afraid that after the joy comes the storm
And that in the end only a dark mirage remains.
It would be so unfair to stifle
Our cry, our ideal taken out of oblivion

Today, the streets are empty again
For a while, the regime has kept its head
And the people have returned home sad and bitter
And in our hearts, it is the silence of the sea.

But we have to say it out loud. So that they know it.
We have marked our history with a stain
A silent people are not sleeping people
No matter how long the night is, the dawn will come.

What we defend will always be immortal
One day, it will take only one spark
And we'll see our balconies and our hearts bloom
With this old flag that refuses to die.

Extrait de *Clameur*

Hocine Tandjaoui

Scène tant de fois revécue, c'est un enfant qui n'a pas encore dix ans, mais qui connaît la radio, avec laquelle il est né et a grandi, comme peu d'enfants de son âge, il en connaît les sons, les voix, les sifflements, les gros boutons et l'œil vert qui maigrit ou grossit au fur et à mesure qu'on s'approche de la station choisie, les crachotements, les notes de musique et parfois les bruitages angoissants de pièces de théâtre radiophoniques à suspense - ces interminables bruits de pas, ceux de l'assassin qui s'approche, ces halètements insupportables des victimes sans défense - oui, l'enfant connaît tout ça, et c'est pour ça que ce matin-là, probablement parce que ses parents interdisent d'allumer la radio le jour - trop cher ?-, donc ce jour-là, l'enfant se trouve chez la voisine, une seconde mère, qui l'autorise souvent à jouer dans son salon, que l'enfant s'approche de la grosse radio à œil vert, une Schneider sans doute, de taille respectable, un meuble avec ses parures de bois verni et ses baguettes de laiton doré, et qu'il entend ce chant, cette voix, cette musique, qui le cloue littéralement au sol, qui le transperce, une voix de femme entre pleur et cri de fête, un ululement fait d'amour, de désespoir et de tendresse. Tu es figé par la force de la révélation, tu es inondé d'un sentiment que tu ne comprends pas, mais auquel tu ne résistes pas, tu es dans la radio, tu es avec elle, avec cette voix, tu es avec ce personnage, son malheur est le tien, comme le tien est le sien, il n'y pas d'autre posture possible, rien d'autre n'est envisageable, tu viens d'intégrer cette voix dans le plus profond de ton être même si c'est la voix la plus mystérieuse qu'il t'ait jamais été donné d'entendre.

L'organisation d'une ville coloniale est d'une affligeante banalité car elle est conçue comme un camp militaire. Prenez une ville tracée les par cohortes de Trajan ou de César, prenez Pompéi, Timgad ou Volubilis, vous y retrouverez le plan des villes coloniales contemporaines, le plan en damier, tracé au cordeau, avec l'obsession de vite l'envahir et de vite l'évacuer, de fluidifier les flux de marchandises, une pensée de fortin et de foirail. En son centre, deux casernes, une église, deux écoles, une synagogue, une mosquée, un square flanqué d'une baraque de loterie et sa gueule cassée, un marché couvert, tous les commerces autour, une rue-bordel, et une multitude de débits de boissons.

Est-ce le miracle de la musique, ou faut-il dire celui de la voix humaine, la voix chantée, est-ce donc ce miracle qui fait qu'un chant, un ensemble de notes, puisse frapper une personne, de façon si juste, si précise, qu'elle en est à ce point bouleversée, qu'elle restera définitivement bouleversée sa vie durant, par ce chant-là, avec la même intensité que la première fois ? Plus encore, chaque fois que tu entends la voix de Dorothy Dandridge, le miracle se renouvelle dans ces retrouvailles, mais il a opéré une autre transformation dans ton esprit : jamais aucune voix de femme ne te sera indifférente. Tu pleures en entendant Janis Joplin, La Callas, Billie Holiday, tu es le frère et l'amant de Nina Simone, et toujours sur le point de te mettre à genoux en écoutant Strange Fruit, *Little Girl Blue* ou *Don't let me be misunderstood*.

Tu n'as pas sept ans et le monde t'explose à la figure. Tu n'as pas sept ans que tu as déjà senti le souffle de la bombe que tu apprendras à nommer plastic -- le souffle, l'onde, les débris, l'odeur, les odeurs mêlés de chair humaine, de sang, de terre et de merde. Tu n'as pas sept ans et tu comprends que le monde est peuplé de tortionnaires et de victimes, les derniers pouvant devenir les premiers, et vice versa. Tu sauras. Tu apprendras à les connaître, les reconnaître immédiatement, à l'instant même où ils rentrent dans ton champ de vision. Tu n'as pas sept ans, non, tu ne les as pas encore, et tu vois des soldats en armes envahir ta maison, brutalisant ton père et ta mère, creuser des trous dans les murs pour trouver les cachettes d'armes, tout détruire sur leur passage. Tu n'as pas sept ans que tu sais lire la rage dans les yeux des soldats n'ayant pas capturé le rebelle. Tu sauras aussi reconnaître la lueur de joie sadique dans les mêmes yeux pour avoir humilié une famille et démoli sa demeure. Tu n'as pas sept ans que tu auras rencontré la lâcheté.

Hocine Tandjaoui is from Biskra, Algeria. His first published poems appeared in 1968 in the Moroccan journal *Souffles*, for which he served as the Algiers correspondent. He is the author of the poetry collection *Le temps de nous-mêmes précédé par L'attente de l'arche* (Paris: Librairie Saint Germain des Près, 1974), and three novels, *Les jours lents* (Paris: Éditions Léo Scheer, 2003), *La bande noire dans l'ombre* (Paris: 108 Édition, 2016), and *Ainsi que tous les hommes (Naples/Tunis/Skopje)* (Paris: 108 Édition, 2020). As a fiction writer, Tandjaoui works with archival sources to recuperate and expand narratives of colonial experience that have been obfuscated by the ideology of global neoliberalism and its attendant historical discourses. This method also informs his semi-autobiographical prose poem *Clameur* (Paris: 108 Édition, 2017). A graduate of the École des Hautes Études en Sciences Sociales, Tandjaoui has worked for several decades in the field of sustainable development in Europe and North Africa. He lives in Paris.

Excerpt from *Clamor*

Translated by Olivia C. Harrison and Teresa Villa-Ignacio

A scene relived so many times: a child, not quite ten years old, but familiar with the radio, with which he was born and grew up like few children of his age, he's familiar with the sounds, the voices, the whistling, the fat buttons and the green eye that gradually thinned or thickened as one approached the chosen station, the sputtering, the musical notes and sometimes the agonizing sound effects of suspenseful radio plays – the interminable steps of the approaching assassin, the intolerable gasps of his defenseless victims – yes, the child knows them all, which is why that morning, probably because his parents forbade him to turn on the radio during the day – too expensive? – that day, the child could be found at the house of a neighbor, a second mother, who often let him play in her living room, the child approached the big radio with its green eye, a Schneider no doubt, a respectably large piece of furniture with its varnished wooden casing and its gilded brass rods, and he heard that song, that voice, that music, which literally nailed him to the floor, which ran through him, a woman's voice between weeping and celebration, an ululation made of love, despair, and tenderness. You're transfixed by the power of the revelation, you're inundated with a feeling you don't understand, but which you don't resist, you're in the radio, you're with her, with that voice, you're with that character, her misfortunes are your own, as yours are hers, no other arrangement is possible, nothing else is imaginable, you have just integrated that voice into the most profound part of your being even though it is the most mysterious voice you have ever heard.

The organization of a colonial city is distressingly banal, for it is conceived as a military camp. Take a city outlined by Trajan's or Caesar's cohorts, take Pompeii, Timgad, or Volubilis: their maps are the maps of contemporary colonial cities, the checkerboard city, drawn in straight lines that betray an obsession with quick invasions and evacuations, optimizing the flow of merchandise, small fort and market square thinking. In its center, two barracks, a church, two schools, a synagogue, a mosque, a square flanked by a lottery shack and the broken-faced WWI veteran tending to it, a covered market, all the shops around it, a brothel-street, and a multitude of watering holes.

Is it the miracle of music, or rather the miracle of the human voice, the singing voice, is this the miracle that song performs, that an ensemble of notes can strike a person so exactly, so precisely, that he is shattered, that he will remain definitively shattered for the rest of his life by that song, as intensely as the first time? What's more, each time you hear the voice of Dorothy Dandridge, the miracle is renewed, but it operates another transformation in your mind: never again will you be indifferent to a woman's voice. You will cry when you hear Janis Joplin, Maria Callas, Billie Holiday, you are the brother and lover of Nina Simone, and you are always on the verge of falling to your knees when listening to 'Strange Fruit,' 'Little Girl Blue,' or 'Don't Let Me Be Misunderstood.'

You are not yet seven years old and the world explodes in your face. You are not yet seven when you feel the blast of the bomb that you will learn to call plastic explosive – the blast, the wave, the debris, the smell, the mixed smells of human flesh, blood, earth, and shit. You are not yet seven and you understand that the world is populated with torturers and victims, that the latter may become the former, and vice versa. You will understand. You will learn to know them, to recognize them immediately, at the very moment they enter your field of vision. You are not yet seven, no, not yet, and you see armed soldiers invade your house, brutalize your father and mother, punch holes in the walls to find where the weapons are hidden, destroy everything in their path. You are not yet seven when you learn to read rage in the eyes of soldiers who haven't been able to capture the rebel. You will also learn to recognize the glow of sadistic joy in the same eyes for having humiliated a family and demolished their home. You are not yet seven when you encounter cowardice for the first time.

Olivia C. Harrison is professor of French and Comparative Literature at the University of Southern California. Her research focuses on postcolonial North African, Middle Eastern, and French literature and film, with a particular emphasis on transcolonial affiliations between writers and intellectuals from the Global South. She is the author of *Natives against Nativism: Antiracism and Indigenous Critique in Postcolonial France* (University of Minnesota Press, 2023), *Transcolonial Maghreb: Imagining Palestine in the Era of Decolonization* (Stanford University Press, 2016), and, with Teresa Villa-Ignacio, co-editor of *Souffles-Anfas: A Critical Anthology from the Moroccan Journal of Culture and Politics* (Stanford University Press, 2016), and Hocine Tandjaoui, *Clamor/Clameur* (Litmus Press, 2021). Her translations include essays and poems by Abdelkebir Khatibi, Jacques Hassoun, Abdellatif Laâbi, Abraham Serfaty, and Hocine Tandjaoui.

Teresa Villa-Ignacio is a literary translator and translation studies scholar whose essays explore ethical and activist motivations in poetic translation. She has co-edited and contributed translations to *Souffles-Anfas: A Critical Anthology from the Moroccan Journal of Culture and Politics* (Stanford University Press, 2016), co-translated the Algerian writer Hocine Tandjaoui's autobiographical prose poem *Clamor/Clameur* (Litmus Press, 2021), and contributed translations to *For an Ineffable Metrics of the Desert*, the selected poems of the Moroccan poet Mostafa Nissabouri (Otis Books/Seismicity Editions, 2018). Her translations of essays and interviews by Tahar Ben Jelloun, André Elbaz, Abdelkébir Khatibi, M'hamed Issiakhem, and Etel Adnan appeared in *Arab Art in the Twentieth Century: Primary Documents* (MOMA, 2018). A Fulbright scholar and NEA Literary Translation fellow, she is associate professor of French and Translation at Kent State University.

From *Clamor/Clameur* by Hocine Tandjaoui, translated by Olivia C. Harrison and Teresa Villa-Ignacio © 2021 (Litmus Press). First published as *Clameur* by Hocine Tandjaoui © 2017 (108 Édition). Reprinted with permission of Litmus Press.

PERSIAN

در میدان

احمد شاملو

آنچه به دید می آید و
آنچه به دیده می گذرد

آن جا که سپاهیان

مشقِ قتال می کنند
گستره ی چمنی می تواند باشد ،
و کودکان
رنگین کمانی
رقصنده و
پُر فریاد

اما آن
که در برابرِ فرمانِ واپسین
لبخند می گشاید ،
تنها
می تواند
لبخندی باشد
در برابرِ «آتش!»[1]

۱۳۵۲

Ahmad Shamlou (1925–2000) was an Iranian poet, considered to be one of the most influential in the modern period. His style builds upon the everyday and the ordinary to convey a revolutionary critique of authority and injustice. He lived and wrote in Iran most of his life.

In the Square

Translated by Maziyar Ghiabi

What comes to sight and
what passes to be seen.

Where the Guards
              execute the task of combat
could be a grassland

and children
              A rainbow
dancing
and screaming.

*

But that
who smiles against the ultimate order
only
can be
a smile
facing "fire!".

1352/1974

Maziyar Ghiabi is a writer and academic, born in Arak, Iran in 1986. He is Wellcome Senior Lecturer in Medical Humanities and Politics at the University of Exeter and the director of the Centre for Persianate and Iranian Studies (CPIS) at the Institute of Arab and Islamic Studies (IAIS). Ghiabi's first monographic book, *Drugs Politics: Managing Disorder in the Islamic Republic of Iran* (Cambridge University Press, 2019), was awarded the Middle Eastern Studies Association (MESA) Nikki Keddie Award for best book on 'revolution, society and/or religion.' Maziyar works in and translates from English, French, Italian, Spanish, Arabic, and Farsi.

ENGLISH

Taking Back Jerusalem

George Abraham

> "I said: you killed me . . . And I forgot, like you, to die."
> —Mahmoud Darwish

Let me be
    brief: by the end of this,
someone will be cursed & I pray it anyone

but Him. Let me start
    again: the night was beautiful but not
romantic. Sure,

there was smoke & moon
    -light. From this angle,
you could almost mistake the city

for *american*. There were 7, all of us born
    of this country before *this* country
existed. It was ours

the way a street cat is mothered
    by thin air. Still, we called this
a reclamation. A taking

back: the sign reading *cameras in use*
    outside an unlit jewelry store,
the palm trees dancing

like they could belong here—city of gravel
    throat & temple's cry—of gold
-blessed forehead & confluenced

histories—how many waters
    anointed & claimed you

inheritance? How many hands

un-sanctuaried you by birth
        -right & con
-quest? A name, however holy,

can be a story of unimaginable
        distance. We could only exit you
by the mouth through which we entered
& there, we first saw Him:
        shadow folded in shadow
speaking hushed & hurried Arabic,

& for the first time that night,
        a familiar I could but couldn't
have known: a Boy with moonlit tongue

promising His mother He'll make it
        back with every breath—peering
around the corner: a soldier, his

gun, that precise small
        -ness—I couldn't unsee him
or Him, couldn't uncast that smile

from his nodding face, our mouths
        pretty with english—he stopped
one of us. & searched

only one of us. & there, I remembered
        my mother, begging God to watch
over us in Jerusalem, where,

at 4 years old, a soldier held a gun
        to her head, & maybe it was or wasn't
at this exact spot, & maybe she prayed

for the wrong son, but in that moment
       I prayed. & there was no God
but the space between us—how the distance

between my holy & His
       holy could resurrect a broken
lord on my breath—& there I began

to understand how my mother could
       abandon her birthright—
& I suppose, she made it out.

Alive, depending on your frame
       of reference. & so did we. & by
some magic, so did that Boy, caught

with the wrong God on His
       breath in his holy city. Forgive me.
I'm trying to understand what makes

one's existence, at a fixed location, a radical
       act—divine even—& what makes
the existence of another, near a specific body

of water, a violence. Forgive me. I wrote this
       in an american airport,
& its magic escaped me.

Taking Back Jerusalem first appeared in *World Literature Today*.

from *Alternate Myths of Exile*

> "Maybe then, a return, maybe wingspan, elsewhere. I am not a proud beast."
> —Zaina Alsous, "A Theory of Birds"

Say instead, the dove returned from the floodwater, bold
-taloned, with a bloodied olive branch, feathers dirtied
        white. The opposite of a murder is a flock

of doves. The opposite of a flock of doves is a genocide. Not all
murders are genocides, but both demand flight. We looked to
wings
        so white, we forgot they raised predatory beings,

& what else could we do but emerge with new lexicon, a truer thing
to call air: we built our Gods from the floodwater & that's
        the story of breath. We were promised

an ocean, but all we wanted was a river's saltless motion.
Hear me: I am writing from a land where survival is no longer
viable. For this, I've tried to apologize, then strike

match to bare earth, but both times I was the one in flames.
I looked into the fire & found, not the absence of God,
        but the opposite of God. & sure, my past tense

implies survival, but before the fire failed at its myth-making,
before a tower rose out from our mistranslations of wind, before
        we filled our boat with a tragic notion of symmetry

to survive those floodwaters, before we told ourselves there was
an Eden to mourn the loss of, we were never skyward beings.
This is what it means for our whole existence to be
an apology. This being the sound our world makes as it rejects
us. This being the sound we make, floating skyward blue: *we did this*
ourselves. We did this to ourselves.

***

I was born a reckoning of
        the historic. Post -human, pre

-image. Imagine me
this way: before a jealous god

siphoned me into mortal, I caught light
        in my bare hands & became it—

tell me heaven is a hilltop to be
        inherited, & I'll say my father crafted me

from liquid thunder, so nothing
        could strip away that God

in me—yes, I once considered Return
        unfathomable, & yes, though it came

at the expense of bodies including
        my own, I Returned anyways; once, a half-

soldier made a labyrinth of my country & I did not
        choke him with golden twine

but with heel pressed to throat because
        it was the softest part of me; once,

I was beheaded, & 3 heads grew back
        in place—a slice where another

one & another one watched me transcend
        my oppressor's recursion—once,

the sun tried to swallow me
        whole, & I grew wings to say, *see me*

eye-to-eye—once, I was unwinged
        but came back re-bodied

in a flurry of blossoms—it is prophecy:
        you cannot kill us when we exist

this loudly. What you call *water*, I call
        ancestor—drown me in that river,

I'll emerge with golden skin—
        suffocate me in my dead, I'll be anything

but sin & when I Returned
        despite everyone

fallen before me—split heel, head
        of snakes un-tethered—my people

looked upon me, open-armed,
        like I was nothing

less than holy, knowing
        it was the prettiest lie: I am,

therefore I parallel—I am,
        therefore, a multitude—so let me be

brief: let me be
>	light—what you call *raising*

hell, I call *reclamation's*
>	*song*—listen: I have lived so many

lives in this body, & there is no greater gift
>	than the sound

your stolen land makes
>	as you ascend back

through its fields, press your palm
>	to its earth, in fracture,

& crown yourself in nothing
>	but its name.

George Abraham is a Palestinian-American poet, performance artist, and writer from Jacksonville, Florida. Their debut poetry collection *Birthright* (Button Poetry, 2020) won the Arab-American Book Award and the Big Other Book Award in Poetry, and was a finalist for the Lambda Literary Award in Bisexual Poetry. They are also the author of the chapbooks *al youm* (The Atlas Review, 2017) and *the specimen's apology* (Sibling Rivalry Press, 2019).

Apologies to All the People in Yemen

Zaina Alsous

after June Jordan

I didn't know and nobody told me and what
could I do or say, anyway?

They said the war is *civil*, they call it *cold*,
bombs rain from an assembled cloud of coalition nations,
they said we have to stop Iran, they said Al-Qaeda, they said ISIS,
most serious journalists cannot assign blame.
Sure, it's been reported more than 50,000 Yemeni children dead,
a dead child for every hour's fraction since the war began.
Sure, Yemeni hospitals have been bombed, in 2015,
and 2016, and 2016, and 2018. In war's heightened fog
mistakes are bound to happen.
Sure, one million people have contracted cholera,
the same illness that appears
in 10 cases a year in the U.S. Sure, international agencies have written
famine and *crisis* in spirals and one report briefly mentions mothers
unable to summon enough milk to fill the mouths of newborns.

Another describes the fate of a mother,
who used to sell boiled eggs in the morning, now
a ceiling of charred blood turned black,
and how do I know the sky I look to at night is not also a ceiling
of charred blood turned black,
and what could I do or say to the memory of this mother,
or the echo of neighbors who shared eggs in the streets of Sana'a?

In American college they taught me to use *it's complicated*,
as a sign of intelligence, anchored against the allure of look.

To turn away from the crater of limbs and say *both sides
both both both both* until it becomes a whisper,

until no one remembers what you were talking about
to begin with. And aren't I an Arab too?
No one told me I would have to choose
between all the faces that could be
my own.

I am not an evil person, just busy explaining
why I deserve to be in this lecture hall, in this living room,
at this desk reading an article about Arab children who die,
on a small plot of theft I can lay claim to.

No one taught me some children are called children
and some would be called *proxies*.

No one told me that Yemen is Gaza is ICE contract is
concentration camp in Florence, Colorado.

Yes, I did know the taxes I paid when buying concealer
to cover the blemishes on my cheek, or on groceries
that kept my belly full, also funded seven thousand and twenty
Paveway bombs. Yes, I voted for the president who authorized
the sale.

But I looked to the streets and they were quiet,
there is so much else to protest, what could I tell people?

And if I could not adequately agitate others to count
the visible ribs of the child dying on the doctor's table,
to hear the screams of light's ending to hold this sound
in a balloon of seething shame, to call this balloon *regulation*,
a refusal of life assignment as gated chlorine,

is it not better to be quiet? I am no expert, I am nobody public.

But I saw the bones, I see them,
even with nobody else around, a wind unfurls and lingers,
it steams off of windows.

The bones are now blinds and all
of the aged cement between bricks and I am sorry.

I'm really, really sorry.

IBIS

1. In France or London, the sibilant machine of SCIENCE invents a bird based on the relics of Egyptian monuments, which is not an exact copy of Nature.

2. Fragments of amber rewoven into the composite IMAGE, is also an invitation to form SOUND, the whistle of species placed in a jar.

3. The jar is the ART of categories, the essential basis of our condition — to not look *away* but to look in wreaths, full blown, to sow our reflection as an exact copy of Nature.

4. According to Herodotus there are two kinds of ibis: black and white, the black is the enemy of serpents, the white is a domestic bird. The afterlife is a house not all birds are allowed in.

5. The best-preserved birds are found in the mummies of Saqqara, wrapped in dyed linen, then sawed open. Tools dressed in membrane correct myth: there were shellfish in the cavities, not snakes.

6. In order to preserve SCIENCE, the language of speculums rusting by the window, we must shake the graves of birds.

7. Shaking graves is not a species complex; which is actually an argument of resemblance, a market for more skin.

8. Precise methods of dissection are also useful when carving the womb out of a woman's corpse. We draw this jar to reproduce ourselves, in order to keep producing the SCIENCE of birds. Bodies are families, bred of facts and secrets waiting to become facts.

9. *She who scrivens —* do you contain a monster nostalgia? *keep keep keep keep keep*

10. Years from now, when sliced open to be redrawn from memory, the naturalists discover an engraving in the urn of my skull: "play dead" (and a laugh track).

Zaina Alsous is a Palestinian-American writer and labor organizer in South Florida. Her debut poetry collection *A Theory of Birds* (University of Arkansas Press, 2019) was awarded the Norma Farber First Book Award, the Etel Adnan Poetry Prize, and the Arab-American Book Award. She is also the author of the chapbook *Lemon Effigies* (Anhinga Press, 2017).

The Worst Ghosts

Hala Alyan

A thing must have hands

                      [to mourn]

what it cannot touch
~
Define in, I say when anyone asks if I've ever been in a war. I smoked pot with a guy I'd known for ages. I slept through the airport bombing. When the window facing the road shattered, I kept a piece in my mother's glove compartment.
~
Sometimes I'll make myself thin

                      [enough]

to slip through walls
~
                      [But if you don't name the tree]

My grandmother's couch milks itself into the carpet

                      [how can you love it]
~
Palestine, a name that means
~
The worst ghosts are the ones that don't come back
~
The officer at JFK scans me. My body, ghost-white, flickering on his screen.

Pretty boy. Blue eyes.

Takes my fingerprint and winks.

Cheer up. You're home.

Call Me to Prayer

A cigarette burn on my forearm. Pink and round as a tongue-tip.

There's Beirut when the floods finally come: bits of tinsel and hamburger wrappers floating through the streets. The city glazed like a donut.

~

In a whorehouse a man tells me to go home to my Baba. A cigarette burn on his forearm. Three brothers he buried in Muslim soil.

In Jerusalem, in El Paso, every road repeats its own Bible name.

~

The towers. Five thousand six hundred and seventy-five miles later, the tunnels.

In the exile's suitcase, a carpet of dead grass. Seven persimmons. A dandelion stem skinny as a grenade pin.

~

All night the wind muscles through the cypress trees, calls me to prayer with the bees.

There is no God but God. This is mountain country, this is evacuation country, this is land of American shrapnel and strip clubs.

No god but.

~

In a night trimmed with moon, lovers kiss their dead like lovers.

Hala Alyan is a Palestinian-American writer, poet, and clinical psychologist who specializes in trauma, addiction, and cross-cultural behavior. Her writing covers aspects of identity and the effects of displacement, particularly within the Palestinian diaspora. She is the author of two novels and several collections of poetry.

November

Sara Elkamel

Before it was a field hospital, this hospital
was a flower shop. Ghost white

filler flowers clustered in every corner
like stars; languished in the lungs of noon.

Now the flower shop is an eye socket.
Rubber bullets tore through socket after socket after

socket. Police protocol suggests aiming
for people's legs. Ingenious, the Eye Sniper

shot at our eyes. In some language, a wild flower
is a bastard, an evil spirit alive in the field.

Outside the hospital that once was a flower
shop, our chorus cursed the sniper and the blind.

Eye go out in search of June. Who will look winter
dead in the eye? Look. A field of sunflowers,

in some language, worshipping the sun.
Before it was a monument, this poem

was a body. Outside the poem, our bodies thaw
in pools around our legs. What stars, where?

This poem first appeared in *The Adroit Journal*.

Drone Fiction

It is possible for funerals
to happen outside windows, possible

for you to watch one proceed
without really going anywhere. Possible for skies

to turn pink and men to hide
behind depths of dust

or black umbrellas the size of clouds.
Possible to go back to the past

and stand behind glass with you,
shout things at the heads that crown

the tarmac, all of us confusing
one dead man for another.

Down, down with _____
_____ did not die
_____ did not die
_____ did not die

To give _____ my life
would be too little. Possible?

To curse the _____
and watch the dead turn to gold.

Sara Elkamel is a poet, journalist, and translator based in Cairo. She holds an MA in arts journalism from Columbia University, and an MFA in poetry from New York University. Elkamel's poems have appeared in *Poetry Magazine*, *Ploughshares*, *The Iowa Review*, *The Yale Review*, *Gulf Coast*, among others. She was named the winner of Redivider's 2021 Blurred Genre Contest, the Tinderbox's 2022 Brett Elizabeth Jenkins Poetry Prize, the Michigan Quarterly Review's 2022 Goldstein Poetry Prize, and she is the recipient of a Pushcart Prize. Elkamel's debut chapbook Field of No Justice was published by the African Poetry Book Fund & Akashic Books in 2021.

"Drone Fiction" first appeared in *20.35 Africa: An Anthology of Contemporary Poetry, Volume 2* (November 2019).

daughterland

K. Eltinaé

On August 15th 2018, twenty-four school children drowned on their way to school near Meroe, Sudan when their boat's engine capsized in a strong current during flooding season. Most of the children onboard were girls. Some families lost all their children.

Because every seed was planted ﻢ by a god or man
who thought himself one
all we have ever passed down
to survive
is war.

What happened to that dagger
you buried outside in case they showed up
to steal your mother-tongue?
that خ in your first name
that slit throats until danger passed.

                       ي was a boat

carrying school children
who were only taught
to swim on land.
Twenty-four
one for every hour and sky I look out at

                                              ر

They are half moons   everywhere
even under my eyes in the morning.
My hands cup water that travels down wrong,
people   stare on as I choke.

ام can be mother
or a spinning head.
Sometimes you have to choose between
weeping in the lap of a stranger
or a compass.

malexi dawa bay

i moved here when اسماء في حياتنا went off the air. floating across the room at some Parisian rooftop terrace party overhearing my old self explain that i come from a country where if you disagreed with the regime they put you on a plane and made you disappear as a way of introduction. sometimes i am mistaken for Cuban or Indian when i meet other brown people. i become their country offering rice and empanadas dancing bachata until the fajr prayer sounds. there are pieces i shed in an airport in Milan to board a cheapass flight. valuables i left with sylvia who had no choice but to leave'em behind. i am always smoking barefoot in my dreams. inbox full of apologies from names i need the yearbook to consult. my pale and freckled secretary types out generic replies. *truly* have *no memory* of that rumor you started in the boys bathroom or your handwriting, just the ugly way everyone knew better and made sure i heard about it. it's the late 2000's but mama forgets sometimes and still says *what will people say?* after lunch we walk back together to where they are all buried now. their pickled tongues strung like sundried tomatoes. still not the season for brunch in the garden for kaftans and kachimba and vicki moscholiou crooning about a love that only exists in songs. you are sorry now because your child doesn't fit or maybe your guilt feels complicit I love that for you... for you i built a wide exit out of that narrow bruise of a past now you're following my news and googling *where is malexi dawa bay?* every year my sister and i would go back for retakes with the school photographer. she couldn't keep her eyes open and I would smile too hard. *don't* mother says over his english instructions. *think of the deer in the lion's jaw, and decide who you are for yourself.*

K. Eltinaé is a Sudanese poet of Nubian/Mediterranean descent, raised internationally as a third culture kid. His work has appeared in *World Literature Today, The Ordinary Chaos of Being Human: Many Muslim Worlds* (Penguin), *The African American Review, About Place Journal*, among others. His debut collection *The Moral Judgement of Butterflies* won The Beverly Prize for International Literature 2019 (BSPG Press). He is the first-place poetry winner of Muftah's Creative Writing Competition *At Home in the World*, the winner of the *Memorial Reza Abdoh Poetry Prize* 2021 from Tofu Ink Press and the co-winner of the 2019 *Dignity Not Detention* Prize from Poetry International.

"daughterland" first appeared as part of 22, the creative anthology by the Liverpool Arts Festival, January 2022. "malexi dawa bay" first appeared in *Rowayat*, issue 6, 2023.

Libya is Blue

Farrah Fray

Gaddafi was captured mid siesta;
he'd tried to escape in a Peugeot truck
the colour of the sky
with a flashing faulty indicator light
shouting "Those damn rats!"
when he stepped outside

but we wanted to be
like Omar Al Mukhtar,
Etched into the azure of ten dinars
Instead, we buy oil for ten times its cost
And dance to Shakira, our shirts embossed
"MILANO"
All we have are our scars racing cars
And coins that jiggle like children's giggles
for the timid young guy who sells dates
out of the back of his Peugeot truck
on the corner of the squares and streets
We were told not to protest on
crisscrossed roads,
An obituary to many
Wanting to be
free
Searching for Libya.

Farrah Fray is an educator and writer living in London. She writes about the experience of being a woman and the missing pieces we get from places and people.

A Fidel

Maziyar Ghiabi

I

I think of the Sierra Maestra
Its air perhaps not so distant
From the afternoon muggy heat
Of the Pianura Padana.

TO get rid of the insects' torment
The steam, not of the saline sea,
But of tobacco, a mixture odorous
Of bodily sweat, foliage, straw, resin and rain,
And lit solely by the truer idea
Of the countryside's smell
By the pork taste of the evening.

IT's the gamble with (hi)story
The hazard of the scribe
Who notes the word that wasn't read:
That Habana seemed surely farther
And therefore more ideal
Of all our Romes
Which too are as she had been:
Mean, pusillanimous and pimp.

AT times a change in style is needed
For to speak the contumacy of bare feet
The escape away from sirens
The joy of the drunken chimeras
That whole of folks we call people.

THUS came that moment
When ink meets the (hi)story page,

In a countryside recovered muggy as before,
Filled with glory – vain and virulent,
Of adrelanic craze
Which is called Revolution!

(Or as would want they,
Apologists of the other-yesterday
The nostalgics of today,
Simple riot?)

II

OF Fidel I envy
The permanent anxiety *en la lucha*
His lucid folly
But more than any other envy
The organising fantasy of the collective gesture.

For me was a revolution in that dance
Teetering of a pontoon
That suspension half-air in a jeep.
Of the *Lider* I envy nothing
If not the benediction of Fate
Against the sorceries of the spies,
And that victory of ours all,
Marble incision in the sand,
In the Bay against the Pigs.

CONTRARILY to any form of the future,
The red Caribbean colour of the revolution remains scanned.
Death does not belong to it,
Yet it persecutes day as night.
The still off morning
remains the time of revolution,
All suffused of dream, sleep and
Trembling vision.

TIME may have stopped in Cuba
To allow not an ultimate barbarity
A last capital tragedy,
In which screens take life
The word is digital
And the creased skin,
by-product of capital.

Calligraphy for a Sagittarius
Fady Joudah

1.

Daily I think of you. Work
pours on my head as people fall

off their lands and out with them.
Dogged bodies that declare themselves

medicinal. Even hospice is a dollar sign,
and my recent exhaustion is

because a woman, colleague of mine, suffered
a pregnancy that forced her off her feet.

The schedule has a hole the size of labor.
My God, even a placenta invades the uterus.

2.

Placenta, "blueberries in leather casing," I say,
and you say, "a burnt out sunflower

by the dark sanguine heat of the womb."
Our conversation pauses for weeks.

Your blood pressure rises with the revolt
in the streets of a country you can't call yours

but want to, as asymptotic echo
or digital upgrade expatriates the world:

We're children in parallel play. I'm here,
and over there the revolt's no dog
of your fighting years.

3.

This numberless numbering of a life
unforgettably forgettable. When again we speak,

it's of your Arabic and of Arabic itself.
Allen was a wolf who listened to a saint

then informed one, we agree, and was the wolf
who shared a meal with Buhturi

across fire and smoke in Iraq
twelve centuries ago. He might as well

have been Chief Guipago
of the Kiowa plains.

4.

Resurrection is our coma in orbit,
or coma in orbit is our resurrection:

near the sun we sublime.
As if graves are a masquerade,

our words are a greenhouse gas
we circulate. Alive with Latin,

for example, we refuse
to let a language die.

5.

I, too, spoke Arabic once,
learned love in it, found love
in the English others see as theirs.
This is what I meant by listening:

how couldn't it be a thousand times
that my voice walked by you blind.

Your Arabic is beautiful,
so sing.

Fady Joudah is the author of five collections of poems: *The Earth in the Attic; Alight; Textu; Footnotes in the Order of Disappearance;* and, most recently, *Tethered to Stars.* He has translated several collections of poetry from the Arabic and is the co-editor and co-founder of the Etel Adnan Poetry Prize. He lives in Houston and practices internal medicine.

Hurra bint Hurra[5]

Mohja Kahf

For the women of Banyas who blocked the highway on April 13th, 2011

I declare [elderwoman faces camera
womencrowd parts]
in the name of the merciful God
I'm from free Banyas
I am a free woman daughter of a free woman
Child of the free I am
Ana hurra bint hurra
[her voice rheumatic, jangling
like any tremorous alert
great-grandmother]
Banyas ahali, Banyas communities,
we're being hemmed in
[counts off on fingers]
Ras al-Nabe3, hemmed in
Old and young, hemmed in
Telephones, they've cut us off
Bread they've cut us off
Water, cut us off. Bread!
Children, they've taken
They're cutting off their—
[Our kids, our kids,
her friend presses].
Everything.
They've not left us a thing
We call out, we're calling out
to the Arab world, to the ahali,

---

5. Video on which poem is based (poem is basically a translation of the *Hurra*'s speech): http://www.youtube.com/watch?NR=1&v=WsJSu88ylEY

to Latakia communities,
Aleppo communities, Damascus communities
[clangor] for the communities of Banyas the free
All you free young folk, come
Banyas will live, will live
Banyas will live free
God is greater [than all who oppress]

The Freedom You Want

"Freedom?" the doctor mutters
over the wounded protester
"Is this the freedom you want?"
without anesthetic without permission
slicing her belly
The doctor is a Baath Party member
and the hospital belongs to the state
But she is a human being
and words belong to her
Outside her window the president
on a billboard says "Freedom
is being safe from terrorists"
On my screen the dissident of another country
who has never set foot in Syria
yips "Freedom in Syria is just code
for imperialist intervention"
I used to believe him
until I met her
and let her guide my hand across her bellyscar

Mohja Kahf was born in Damascus, Syria. Her family moved to the United States in 1971, and Kahf grew up in the Midwest. She earned a Ph.D. in comparative literature from Rutgers University and is the author of the poetry collections *Hagar Poems* (2016) and *Emails from Scheherazad* (2003) and the novel *The Girl in the Tangerine Scarf* (2006). Her poetry collection *"My Lover Feeds Me Grapefruit"* was published in 2020.

"The Freedom You Want" was first published in *The Markaz Review*, 14 March 2021

Where This Fire Begins
Ismail Khalidi

with squads of black-clad assassins
bellowing fire from their chests
on fundamentalist oriental
spaghetti western sets?

is that really where we will begin?
or with a raucous foot stomp-
ululation - lamb slaughter - wedding party
made funeral
on the turn of a dime
by projectiles severing time
from above?

what about with the two jets
slamming two towers
one morning?

a protest?
          revolution?
                    a civil war?

what about with some chap in London
and his counterpart from Paris
drawing maps over drinks
dividing up their wogs
dapper turn of the century Gods?

but these are not equal things
and who here cares
that in Arabic we say *books*

are written in Cairo,
published in Beirut
and read in Baghdad

and are such things even true anymore?

and what about those cities
 that I loved, even from afar?
who here will mourn
those places
and their disappeared?

where do we start this story?
where do we start the clock?
how do we know
where this fire begins
and where it stops?

*

something is born, a gnawing,
an answer of sorts
on a wet grey Tuesday
when everything is gravity
on the other side of this window
overlooking the S train as it shuttles
its settlers over invisible lines

today I am struck by the fact
that the muezzin is not on call here
which should not be a surprise after all
these decades

and yet in his place
only a metallic silence

as the hour for evening prayer comes and goes
in this Northern tumor, this place
full of hard honeycombs
built for humans to die in.

I don't even pray
never did, but there it is anyway
echoing over the rooftops
just for me
        like a phantom limb or a dead twin
        whose presence one can sense
calling me
to my knees

but it's only the bark of car horns
and that milky albino pit-bull
left alone in the courtyard below
always
slippery with darkness

and at this moment I want nothing more
than to play the Oud;

to belt out
some nomadic Damascene dirge,
some Baghdadi lament or fugue,
some San'aani song or ancient poem

that rings with defiance and defeat
unrequited love, horses and desert moons
and beautiful shit like that

maybe then, I think, I'd feel
more human, more there
than here

but I have no Oud
and I can't carry a tune
to save my life
let alone to save the smiles
of a couple million Arabs
here or there, give or take, more
or less

but the air doesn't lift the sound
of 12-strings here anyway

not like it does where figs and almonds grow,
where gazelles can sometimes be seen
and where men gel their hair and hold hands
and think nothing of it
rapping about football and politics and love

and darkness is everywhere now

and there is no more Spring to speak of
so my chorus comes into focus:

> *the ancient cities lay hollowed*
> *and there is no one*
> *left to root for*
>
> *There is no one left*
> *to root for*

there is only God-talk
red lines tracing the night,
tyrants and strutting beards, proxies
and paymasters in capitals far

from the sounds of windpipes and arteries
announcing the end of things
on the ground

a fight outside brings me back
to Brooklyn where two rats
must have eyed the same bone
and that half bodega bagel bloated
with rain since last Wednesday

one speaks
in broken English, the other
a language I have never heard

it is settled, then;

tomorrow I will buy an 'oud,
tomorrow I will sing the blues

Ismail Khalidi was born in Beirut to Palestinian parents and raised in Chicago. He is a playwright and director who has written, directed, performed, curated, and taught internationally. Khalidi's plays include *Tennis in Nablus* (Alliance Theatre, 2010), *Truth Serum Blues* (Pangea World Theater, 2005), *Foot* (Teatro Amal, 2016-17), *Sabra Falling* (Pangea World Theater, 2017), *Returning to Haifa* (Finborough Theatre, 2018), and *Dead Are My People* (Noor Theatre, 2019). He is the editor of *Inside/Outside: Six Plays from Palestine and the Diaspora* (TCG, 2015) and *Mizna: The Palestine Issue* (Winter 2019).

OCCUPATION (AN INDEX)

Khaled Mattawa

> *who is the human in this place,*
> *the thing that is dragged or the dragger?*
> — Lucille Clifton

A.

A day's living—
hands' cunning
drained

A murdered son
for cameras
to retain

A taker with
no pang
of guilt

A slave
who has made
a mistake

A song made
to induce
survival

A victim,
it's your turn
now

Air that shepherds
jet fighters,
missiles, drones

Amicable people
with whom we are
on equal terms

Amused our-
selves counting
the dead

An apricot tree
laden
with fruit

And the pastures
at Lafwat
bursting green

Arms bound,
patience withers,
no livelihood

Armed
vehicles, tanks,
crushed cars

As if the land
had no
people

Ask no questions
and you'll hear
no lies

At the shiver
of spring
in the grass

B.

Barbed wire
looped around
huts and tents

Bestial sexual
license of occupied
people

Blaring from
the soldiers'
loud speakers

Brainless
elites, degraded
masses

Breaking
of fingers
and knees

Bulldozers
cut down a row
of cypresses

Burnt corpses
on both sides
of the road

Burying
the living
for sport

C.

Carrying filth,
wood and water—
a low life indeed

Carrying on
as if free
of disease

Chased them
from before
the city gate

Climb back
to the clouds,
O beloved water

D.

Degenerates
who deserve to
be conquered

Destroyed all
that belongs
to their jinn.

Dig out olive
trees, burn
lentil fields

Disfigure past
to paralyze
imagination

Dreams that
pine for
lost sleep

Drink you in
heaving gulps,
beloved water

E.

Entropy
undertaken
with courage

Essential duplicity
of occupied
people

Even managed
to defecate into a
photocopier

Everyday a story
about why they're
killing you

Exchanged
in a market
of guilt

F.
Finish the
population
exchange

For months
the curfew
closes doors

For weeks
for four or five
hours a day

Force is
all they ever
understand

Forced to leave
homes, move in
with family

Forgive them
for forcing us to
kill their children

G.

Garments up
around their
waists

Gunned down
in the forced
labor camp

H.

How do
you master
innocence

How do you
spin your
pleading

How high
must the
walls rise

How long will
the roads be
yours alone

How long will
you wish they'd
just disappear

How will you
explain to
your children

How you've
crept into
our lungs

I.

I have no
illness but
this place

I myself had
to become
a weapon

I remember
those places,
forget my loss

I wish
I were
there now

If I were one
of them, I'd be
a terrorist too

If you
deserve our
confidence

I'll be grateful
to reach them
alive

Imprisoned
clan, banished
kin's abode

In drawers
they pulled
out of desk

Into plastic
bags, they
scattered

J.

Jailing
by old
Jailliol

Joints of their
limbs like knots
in a rope

Jolly
pioneers
of progress

Joy, sorrow,
devotion,
rage—

Just an accident
arising from the
weakness of others

Just as though
a mission
to civilize you

Just robbery
and murder
on a great scale

Just the thought
of their humanity—
like yours

K.

Keep
hope
intact

Keep plunder
and livestock
for yourself

L.

Like drugged
cockroaches
in a bottle

Lives lost
before
my eyes

M.

Malnutrition
permanently
introduced

Man who
wants to move
forward

Many
without
a story

Millions
torn from
their gods

Monster, the
everyday
monster

More effective
and efficient
tyranny

Most
unscrupulous
financiers

Mutual
services
and complicity

Must believe
myself
superior

N.

Neighborhood
dogs join
in the ruckus

No colonization
without eviction
and expropriation

No illness but
a providence
of grief

No illness but
"Beat them!
No pardon"

No illness but
the drip
of loss

Not one
drop
of blood

Not one
effort, not one
privation

Not only
pathological
but pathogenic

Now a field
hand on my
own land

Now a morsel
to shove down
a throat

O.

O civilization:
innocence
misunderstood

O killer,
needful
of dead love

On children's
hair, faces,
into their mouths

On the floors,
in emptied
flowerpots

Open hands
snuffed out
like flames

Open hands
that kept
opening

P.

Perform
your ablutions
then return

Pioneers
who deserve
admiration

Pioneers who
made the
desert green

Propensity for
violence (among
occupied people)

Puddles hold,
and gusts of
wind release

Q.

Questions in
the interests
of science

Quick glance
of unconcerned
wisdom

Quickly enough
when the flesh
falls off

Quirky tweaking
of our private
will

R.

Remains of
a suicide
bomber

S.

Sacrifice
given despite
perseverance

Sand bag
terraces,
hunker down

Scattered
in cardboard
boxes

Set it on
fire when
you're done

Silver and
gold, trays
of brass

Soldiers' piss
like blood,
falling warm

T.

The bullet
in her riddled
heart

The crowning
glory of
our genius

The rot
of loved ones'
corpses

The soldiers
take over
the roof

Their orange
groves
burned

There are no
innocents
here

They defecate
in kitchen sinks,
in pots and pans

They defecate
on computers,
on children's beds

They want you
to bow like
a slave

This is how
you make
the land yours

This was
policy not
a joke

To bring you
up to
modernity

To drive
them out of
our memories

To make
you a new
nation

Truth
stripped of its
cloak of time

U.
Uproot their
pomegranate
trees

Urinated into
dozens of
water bottles

V.
Verging on tears,
he knew
it was a lie

Vets describe
a dark, depraved
enterprise

Vivid, on-the-
record accounts
of slaughter

Voice changed, said:
"We must talk like
civilized people"

Voices that seemed
suspiciously
innocent

W.
Watch your
injury spun
into blame

When your
conscience
is naught

Where your
pain is
priced low

Whimpers
for mercy
into claws

X.
X drawn on
homes to be
demolished

X equal
my right name
and address

Y.
You are
drenched, but
you've survived

You vow again
never to leave
it to them

You become the
cause and effect of
their oppression

Z.
Zealous
patience to heap
and hoard

Zenith to
nadir till
the end

Zero-
tolerance
policy

Zigzagged
running every
which way

Khaled Mattawa is a Libyan poet, and a renowned Arab-American writer. He is also a leading literary translator, focusing on translating Arabic poetry into English.

Lyrics from "I Wish" from the album *Eye Know Faces* (2017)

Omar Offendum

Ay man where you from?

I'm from a place where
revolutions slowly suffocate from sarin gas & selfishness
& freedom's a mirage my people stared up at with helplessness
When SOS alerts were sent, nobody got the messages
& soulless men then learned to turn a profit from the recklessness
Aware of just how short a span humanity's attention is
If the White House is ambivalent
That doesn't mean the Kremlin is
Hindsight is 20/20
Divine right's been claimed by many
And they still don't know Aleppo, let alone what a White Helmet is…

Let's keep it moving
Like Obama with the red lines
Or Trump with the headlines & hairlines
I swear, I'm a rare kind of dude
Like the term for worms in Arabic
Unearth my buried heritage
From cities turning derelict

All that time I had before
I just wish I cherished it

All I can remember now is war
Bilad Al-Sham she perishes

I wish, I wish, I wish I met you at a different time
Suffice it to say, I could've come up with a different rhyme

But glory days are often figments of a stricken mind
Coping mechanisms for whom History hath left behind...
But hey it didn't have to be this way
These songs of freedom ain't naïveté
They were sourced from truths as credible
As regime change is inevitable
I just hope I live to see the day

Omar Offendum is a Syrian-American rapper / spoken word artist. Known for his unique blend of hip-hop and Arabic poetry, he has been featured on prominent world news outlets, lectured at a number of prestigious academic institutions, collaborated with major museums and cultural organizations, and helped raise millions of dollars for various humanitarian relief groups. He was recently named a Kennedy Center Citizen Artist Fellow, an Arab America Foundation "40 Under 40" award recipient, and a member of both the Pillars Fund cohort for Muslim Narrative Change and the RaceForward Butterfly Lab cohort for Immigrant Narrative Strategy.

The Season of the Jasmine Vine

Nadya Tannous

Winter 2016

My favorite jasmine vine is bare
All of its buds and flowers have fallen

I am home. You enter
through the door, the same as always.
Except, you are upset.

The air strikes and regime advances have left you bare.
All the flush from your face has fallen.

Like a flower in harsh weather,
you have wilted before me.

Spring 2016

Then the torment starts

In an old Umayyad palace,
striped walls laced
in pale jasmine

It makes sense it would be here,
a few hours over the border
in Jordan.

Why does this place smell so sweet?

Homesick.
"Syria is in the air"

The essence of
Ghurba غربة
exile from
Aleppo
Hama,
Yarmouk, Damascus
infused by
nostalgia that is
always hungry for stimulus

We take the King's Highway looking for lunch.
You are quiet in the car.
You stare out the window.
You put your face against it and
You drift.

"To where?" I ask you, thinking of food

We are fed by a reminder of
the first mother who fed us.

"To Aleppo" you tell me, dreaming of sustenance

I was worried.
I am always worried
about you.

Rain 2016

The Ceasefire announced itself in a deluge
5 years of your face carved into marble.
I finally saw it crack.

There were 104 documented protests in Syria today.
You tell me.
You are happy.

You are proud.
You are sad
You aren't there.

You let the exclamations slide
off your tongue
You tell of
Resilience
of a people
who
"after 5 years of shelling, and air strikes,
and barrel bombs, and proxy war,
family being killed, and imprisoned,
and living under siege and sanctions
and watching people die from starvation,
and destruction, and pain,
and torture, and drowning
and exile"

And
I saw you smile, hopeful, momentarily
accolades, falling like rain, for the future
and
it was the first time in a long time.

"My people are alive"

Tugging at a new season
like the flowers that grew from dead soil
at the first sign of rain
"My people are alive"

As the hours pass
As your people are being cut back again
like weeds
as news travels
you sigh and

do not say a thing for the rest of the drive home.
The loudest thing we could hear was
the ringing of our own thoughts in our heads
and the
tick tick tick of
the car wheels
driving us back to a place
neither of us considered home.

Summer 2016

And then
You settled back
into the statuesque person you have become.

It is the dry season.

You have been stiffly pacing from your bed to the window box,
to the garden patch and
back to your dark room.

Your face is flush again.
Not dead like in the winter months but
still motionless.

Tomorrow is the first day of summer
in
Amman.
You have found yourself
Surviving

Another season of war and its friends
You call this recent state of events, "Money matter"

Aid, you tell me
is the change

of money from
a solid state, whole to
a liquid state, partial transfer to
a gas, gone finally,
a plasma of
so many people, spilt by the behest of
corruption ionized by
the pockets of greedy middle men
who are warmed by the flames of war which
burn people into vapor

Everyone wanted a piece of Syria

Four Summers ago
You texted me from Sham to let me know that Revolution was not
just on the horizon,
it was in the streets.

All the threads of these stories
Are frayed now
Who can weave a coherent pattern through such devastation and loss
and

Your purpose once was the unshackling of your peoples' imaginations
before hell broke loose instead of
Freedom

Western opportunism and engineered defeat
took up the center piece
where home should have been

And every flower will surely die says the part of yourself you wish
didn't survive

The heat of summer rises with the sun rays, and the rain has totally
vaporized
It is sweltering, even at night

Ramadan points with its fingernail hung in the sky
towards the scarcity of food and resources for the Syrians we see
scattered on the streets of East Amman
Or
Every morning lining the streets of Khalda
with no end in sight

The sun beats down but surely there's a hotter layer of hell

This summer
We feel the pressure
Frazzled

Faith is doing most of the heavy lifting
In fact, the flowers outside still seem very much alive
despite the trying heat
They have not forgotten their original instructions

Through a marathon of months
The jasmine vine is flowering again

As they bloom and then mature, the blossoms turn fragrant
The smell fills the air around our apartment at night
I watch you close your eyes and wait

We must learn our own survival
so we do not become victims of
the time that remains.

The jasmine vine knows this
more intrinsically than we do.

Fall 2016

It's been 5 years.
like this.

Each season replacing the one before it
We smell memories
from before we came to know a home
that existed only in memory.

The jasmine vine is in bloom
fed by
The first mother who feeds us
We will live here
We are alive here
waiting for

Home

may no longer be there
when all this is over.

Nadya Tannous is a community organizer, writer, and researcher born and raised in the Bay Area (Unceded Ohlone Territory). She focuses on refugee rights, intercommunity empowerment, and returning land to the people and people to the land. She is a creative partner of Donkeysaddle Projects and is a member of the Arab.Amp team through Temescal Arts Alliance, and is a founding member of the Ghassan Kanafani Resistance Arts Scholarship. She holds an MSc in Forced Migration and Refugee Studies from the University of Oxford and a BA in Anthropology from UC Santa Cruz.

Miss Sahar Completes Her Application for Travel Documents
Lena Khalaf Tuffaha

1. **You must take with you at least two days' rations**
   I often find myself in this predicament,
   my mouth crowded with farewells. One letter
   dropped for another, from system of meaning
   to nonsense. And in this manner, we upend
   the drudgery of time-telling.

   I have nothing
   to show for my survival.
   I arrive at the precise moment
   of spectacle. My father who died waiting
   did not wish to repeat the story
   of the almonds ripening on the tree,
   of stepping beyond the threshold
   of the house first, because my mother could not,
   or of the clap of her palms
   against her thobe, bewildered
   by the task of choosing what little to carry.

2. **You must have sufficient money for your onward journey**
   There is a word for this, the clatter
   of a life disassembling, prayers
   passing between the already dead
   and the dying who must bury them.
   In the camp, our purpose is to survive
   thirst and rations and waiting
   on the verge.

3. **You must see that your travel document is filled out completely, no item can be left out**
   Prayer for the Dead:
   Blessed be those who are buried in their homeland

>Prayer for Those Who Might Yet Die:
>Blessed be those who carry the keys to their homes wrapped in linens
>Prayer for the Dying Burying Their Dead:
>Blessed be those who do not outlive their children.
>Prayer for Its Own Sake:
>Spare us any more of these blessings.

4. **If any of your party are over twelve years of age, they must have a separate document with their photo on it**

>I tell the students, if you forego
>the diacritic marks, one hundred
>can sound like death or like water.
>These papers claim us
>for no one but the crossing.
>The beginning and the end
>will be no different.

5. **You are not allowed to carry gold**

>In the camp, I learned an alphabet
>for singing. The women who taught us
>were younger than our mothers,
>and we aged together. Our rations
>were flour and oil and the poems
>stitched into the linings
>of our uniforms. Bite down on these verses,
>they will not tarnish. Weigh them
>at the jeweler's shop in the city.
>A people cannot survive on bread
>and gunpowder alone.

6. **You are not allowed to carry any letters for persons residing outside Palestine.**

>Letter to the Interior:
>
>They have always known our name.

7. Your baggage may not exceed sixty kilos

> I want nothing from this holding station.
> My mother left
> the kettle on the stove. There is
> a lemon tree, she tells me, behind the window
> and always mint in the garden.
> Every road in our village will be
> wide enough for us to walk side by side.
> What could I need
> that is not already there?

8. You must report to the nearest police office within twenty four hours of arrival at destination

Where were you born

                              Do you speak the language

Where was your father born
What is your father's name
What is your grandfather's name
What is his father

                                          Are you now

Where was your mother

                             Or have you ever been

Where is it on a map

                             nostalgic for their childhood

Do you have anything to declare
Do you have anything left to lose
Did you consider the implications of

                                   continuing to survive

Do you recognize the state of

                              affairs that keeps you here

Do you know the number of
                gates you will have to be granted passage through
Do you believe in

                                           an ending

Do you know the location of your village
Did you pack your own

                                onions for the tear gas

Do you recognize any of these

                                                              lost battles

How long do you plan to stay

Can you enunciate

Can you write

                the names and addresses of everyone you know here

Do you understand the laws

                        that make all your responses a provocation

Lena Khalaf Tuffaha is a poet, essayist, and translator. She is the author of three books of poetry, *Water & Salt* (Red Hen Press), winner of the 2018 Washington State Book Award for Poetry, *Kaan and Her Sisters* (Trio House Press, July 2023), and *Something About Living,* winner of the 2022 Akron Prize for Poetry, forthcoming from University of Akron Press, 2024.

"Miss Sahar Completes Her Application for Travel Documents" was previously published by *Crab Creek Review* in 2018 with a different title, and will be published in *Kaan and Her Sisters*, forthcoming in July 2023 by Trio House Press.

People Who Are Trying to Be Polite

Peter Twal

A dog in the dark
shadow of your self-portrait, you
snap off my arm   in black, sight
blurry,   waterboarding me & another & another & *here, I've
saved you*

the last bite of this grenade   I'm not asking
you to survive this
breath of   closet fire,   our bones tangled, braided
smoke clouds overhead   I am asking you to live with me   Even
if that tattoo
won't fit on my face   Even if you don't notice
the fresh pair of lungs   I don every day

These holes I burrow in the thick   sponge before stuffing
my country   between my ribs, its wild

wriggling, a fish
caught in my eyelashes

& this, the cigarette I offer to share
That I'd even take the end on fire

Peter Twal is the author of *Our Earliest Tattoos*. His work has been published widely, and he works as an electrical engineer in Phoenix, Arizona.

To the people of Gaza: at the epicenter of loss, resilience, and human dignity.

To the people of Sudan and Yemen: Forgive us for our silence and inaction.

To all the victims of violence

www.ingramcontent.com/pod-product-compliance
Lightning Source LLC
Chambersburg PA
CBHW041322110426
42743CB00051B/3436